AF606855

HUNTERS IN HIGH HEELS

PHOTOGRAPHS BY
OMAR RODRÍGUEZ-LÓPEZ

EDITED BY STEPH CELAYA

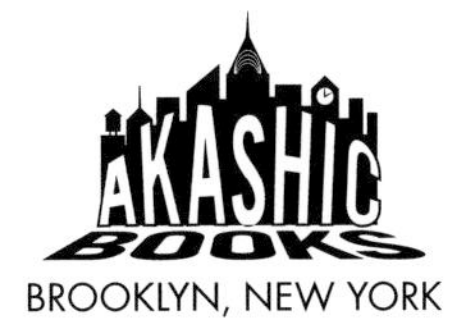

BROOKLYN, NEW YORK

INTRODUCTION

When I met Omar Rodríguez-López in 2015, a camera wasn't one of the instruments I knew him to yield as a tool for expressing his creative vision. Much to my curiosity, but not to my surprise, I found that Omar's art is not limited to expression onstage or in a studio, it also inhabits the visual medium. During our initial conversation, I learned that Omar had an archive of negatives and photographs he had taken over the course of his career. His goal was to have these curated into specific time periods and to then publish them in a book that accurately reflected the time, the place, and the energy of those years. Given that I have spent my life as both a photographer and a photographic agent, we soon realized we spoke the same language. From that point forward, Omar and I were connected on this visual journey. Over the past ten years, *Hunters in High Heels* is a project that has come into focus at its own measured and steady pace.

Omar is deeply interested in the world. As an observer of changing landscapes, shifting cultures, and evolving relationships, his touchstone has become the camera. The combination of his international recognizability and his desire for privacy provides a unique and captivating glimpse into his nomadic life. The irony that Omar Rodríguez-López connects to and captures the quietest moments amid, and in between, some of the loudest places is not lost.

In these photographs, it's clear that there is a gravitational pull for Omar toward the universal visual language that surrounds us. These grounding cords can be found in any country, in any language—highway signs from buses, city skylines from hotel rooms, and cloud views from airplane windows. The only difference with what is also captured through Omar's lens is the destination of these buses and airplanes. It is direct access into the arenas, music video sets, and recording studios with friends and colleagues. This body of work, taken between 2001–2005, is an intimate glimpse into this period of time.

STEPH CELAYA

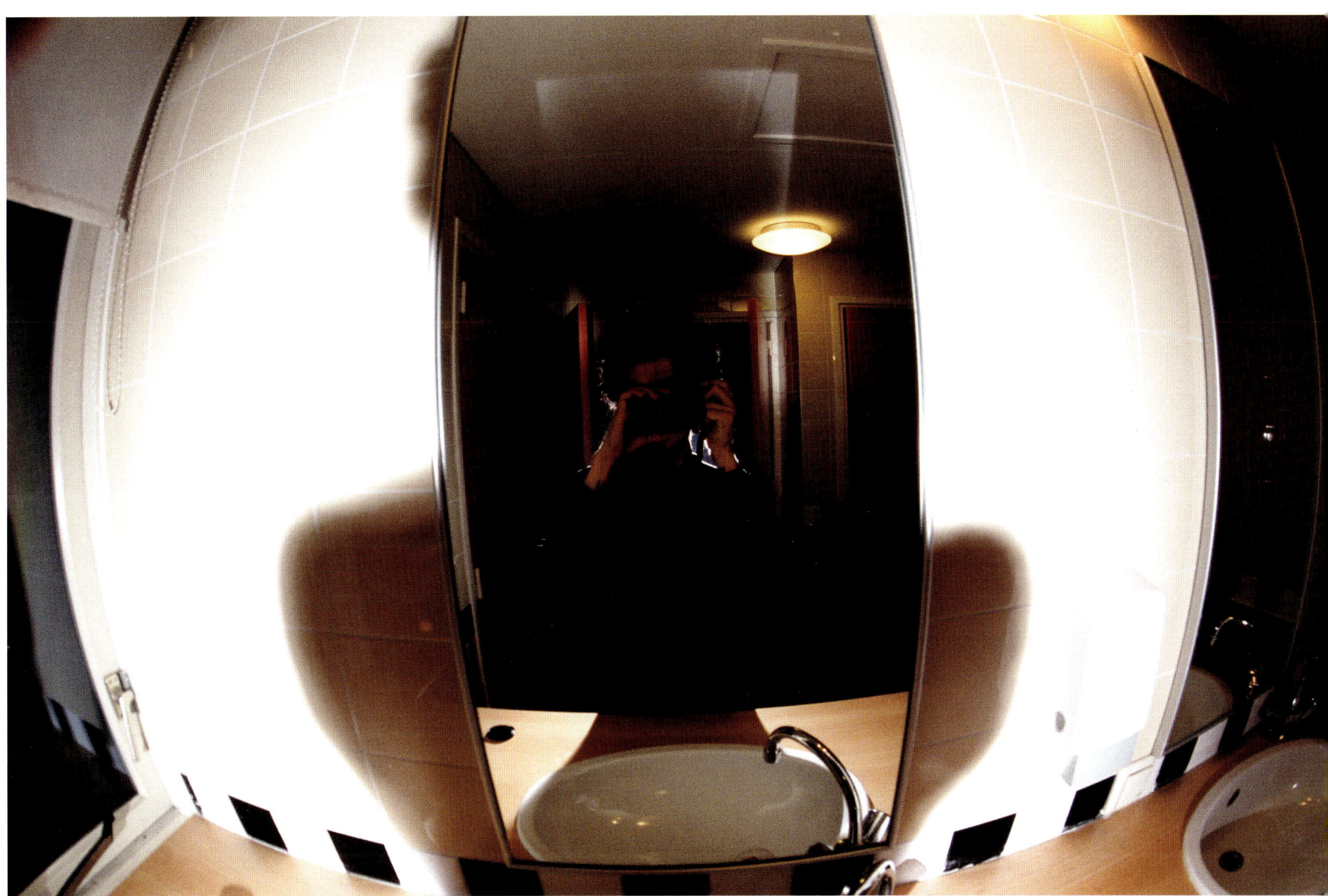

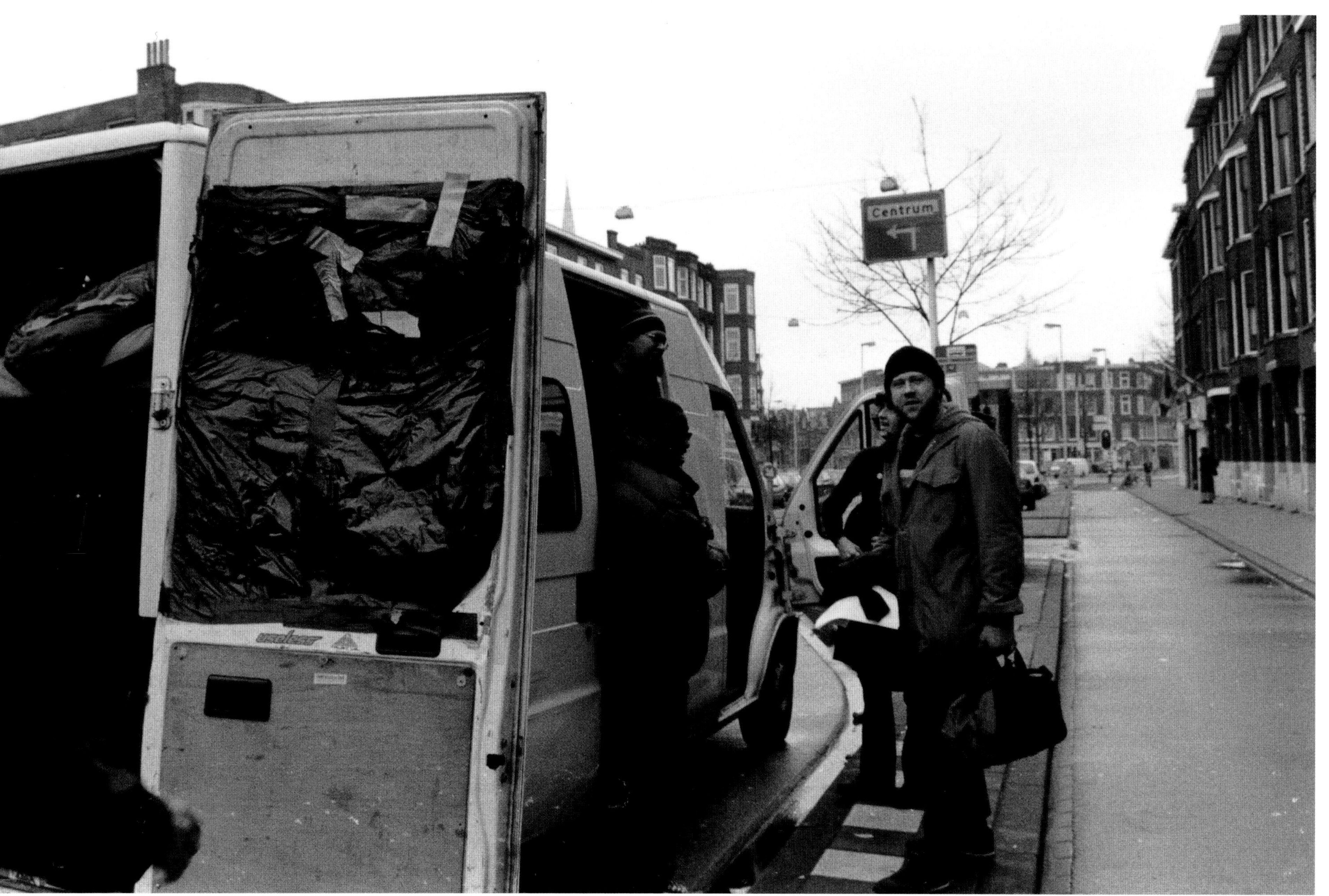
Centrum

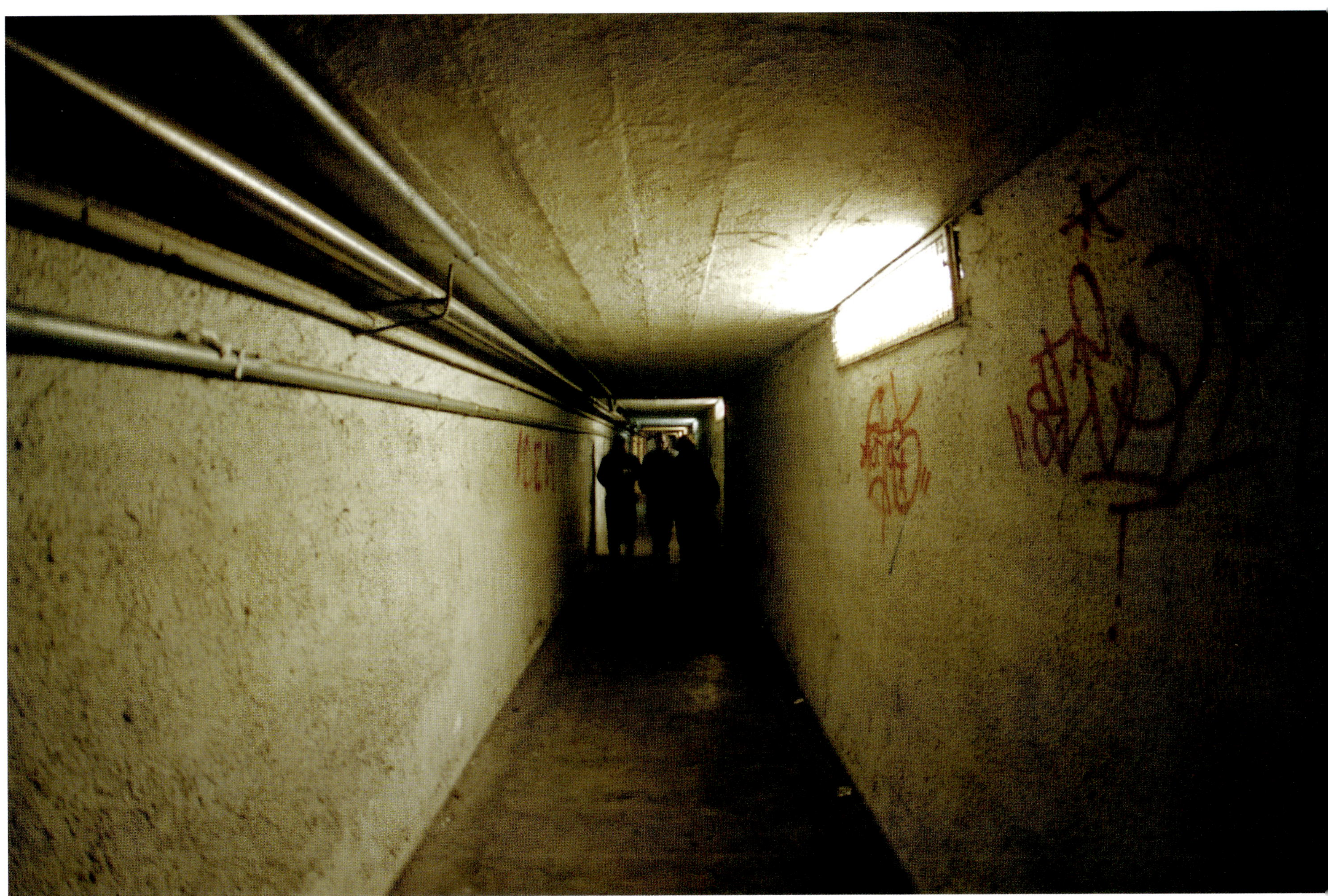

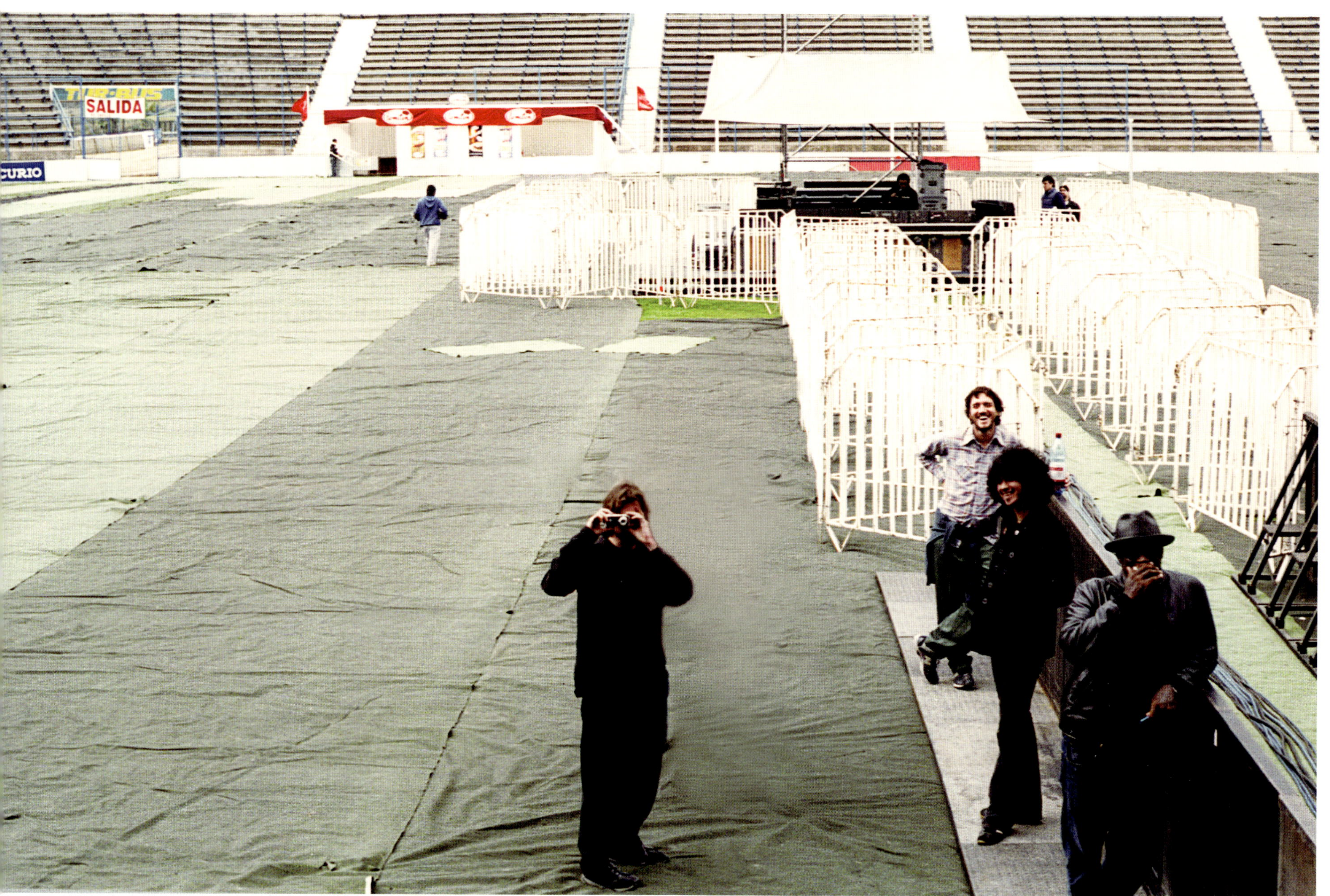
SALIDA
CURIO

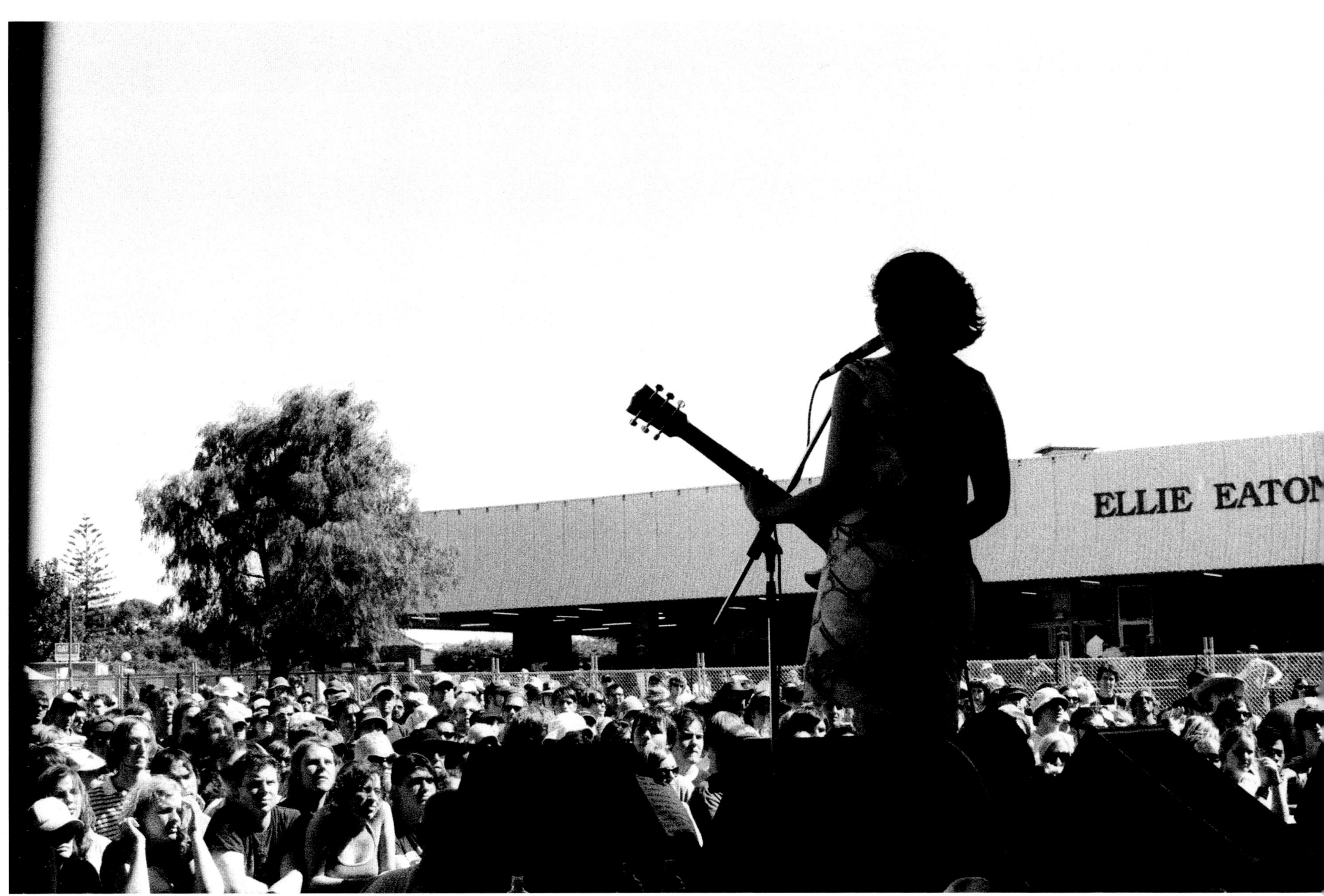
ELLIE

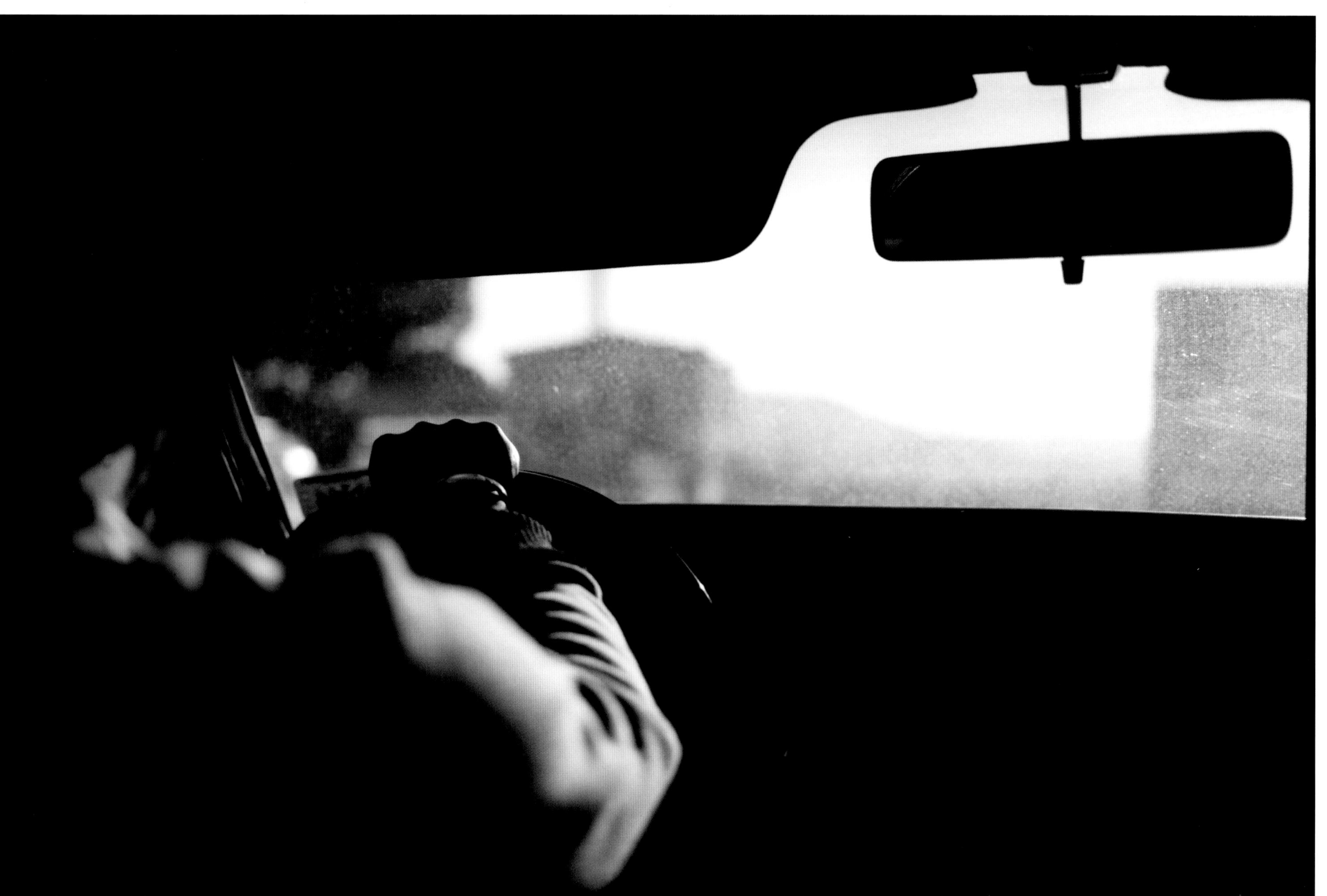

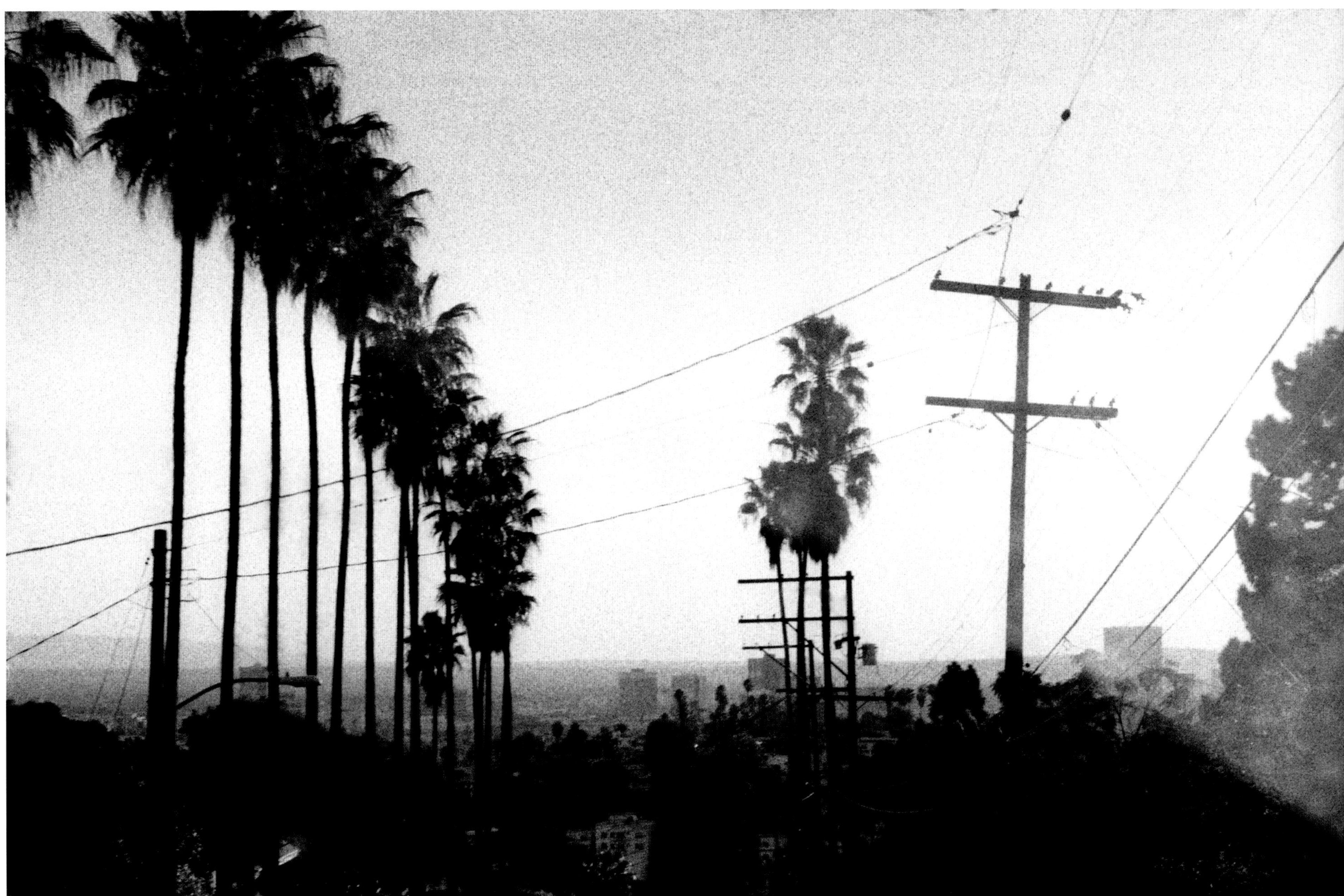

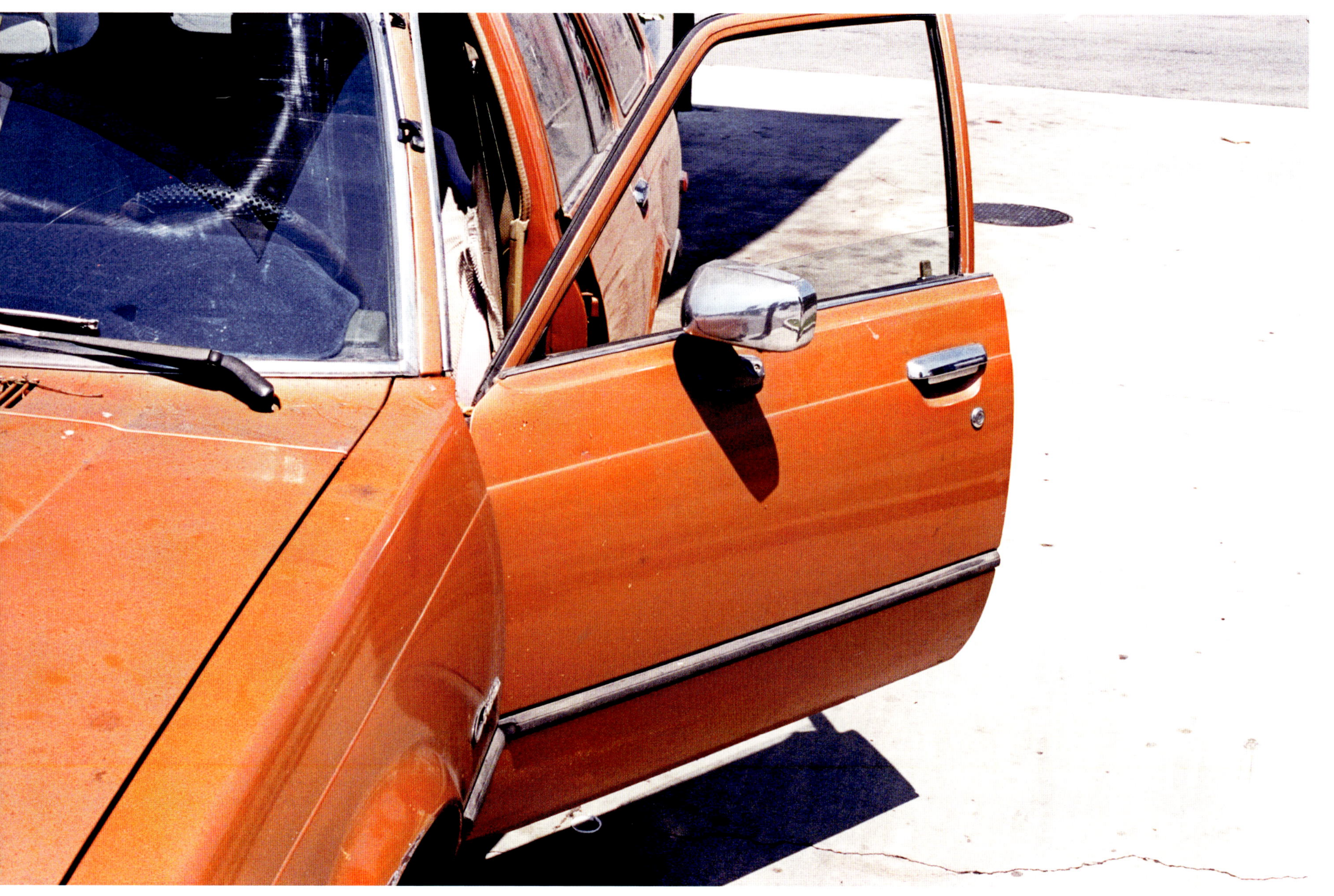

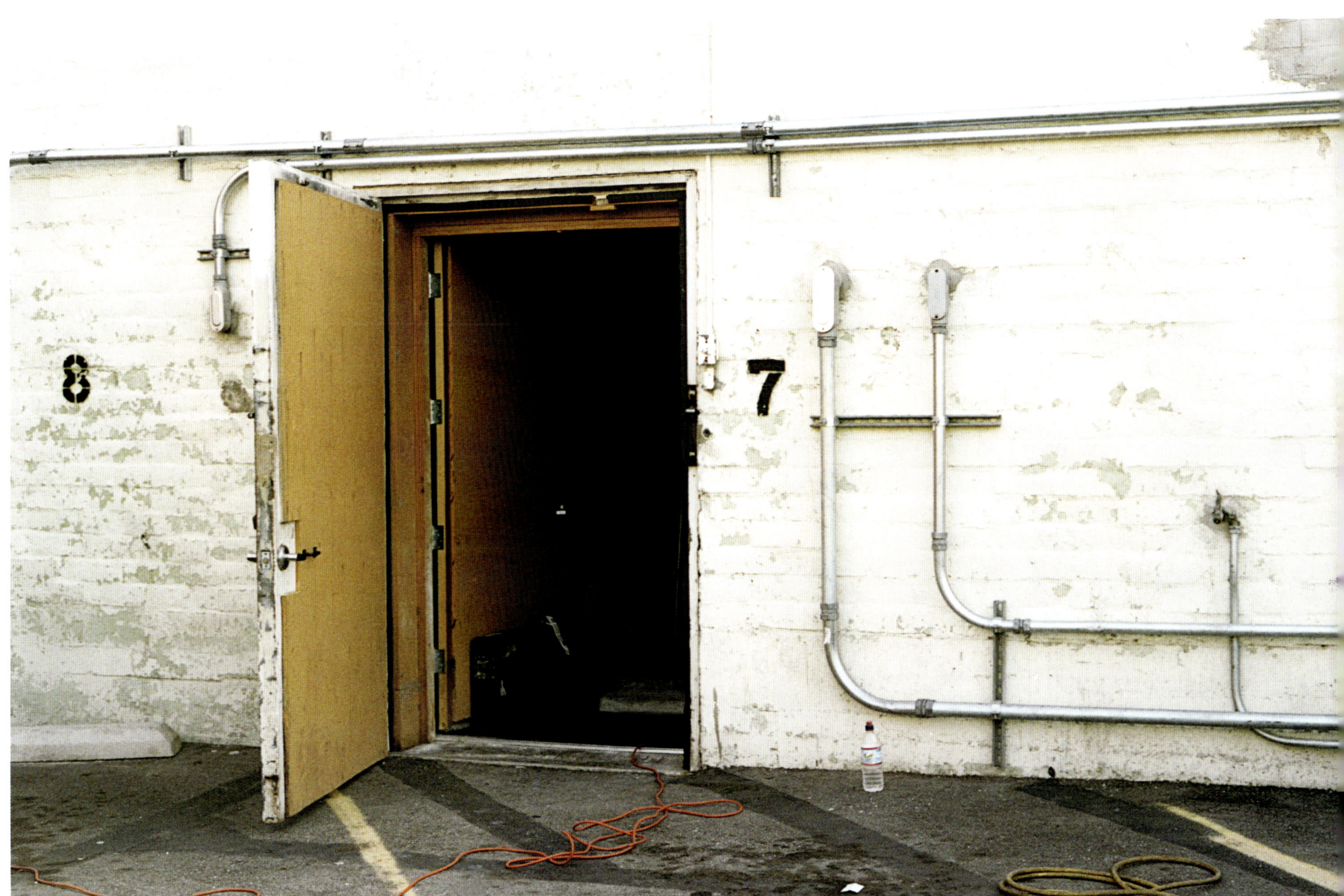
8
7

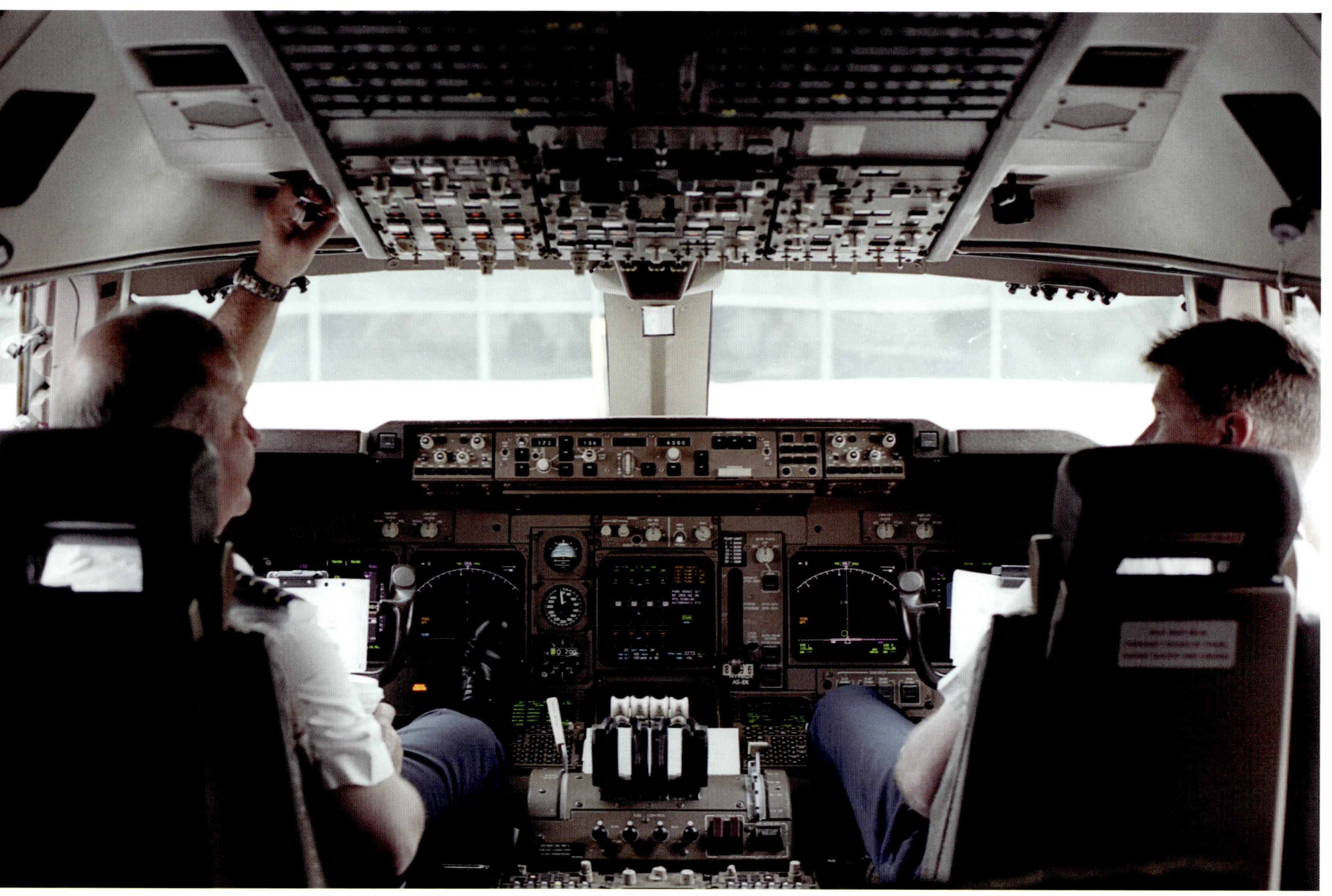

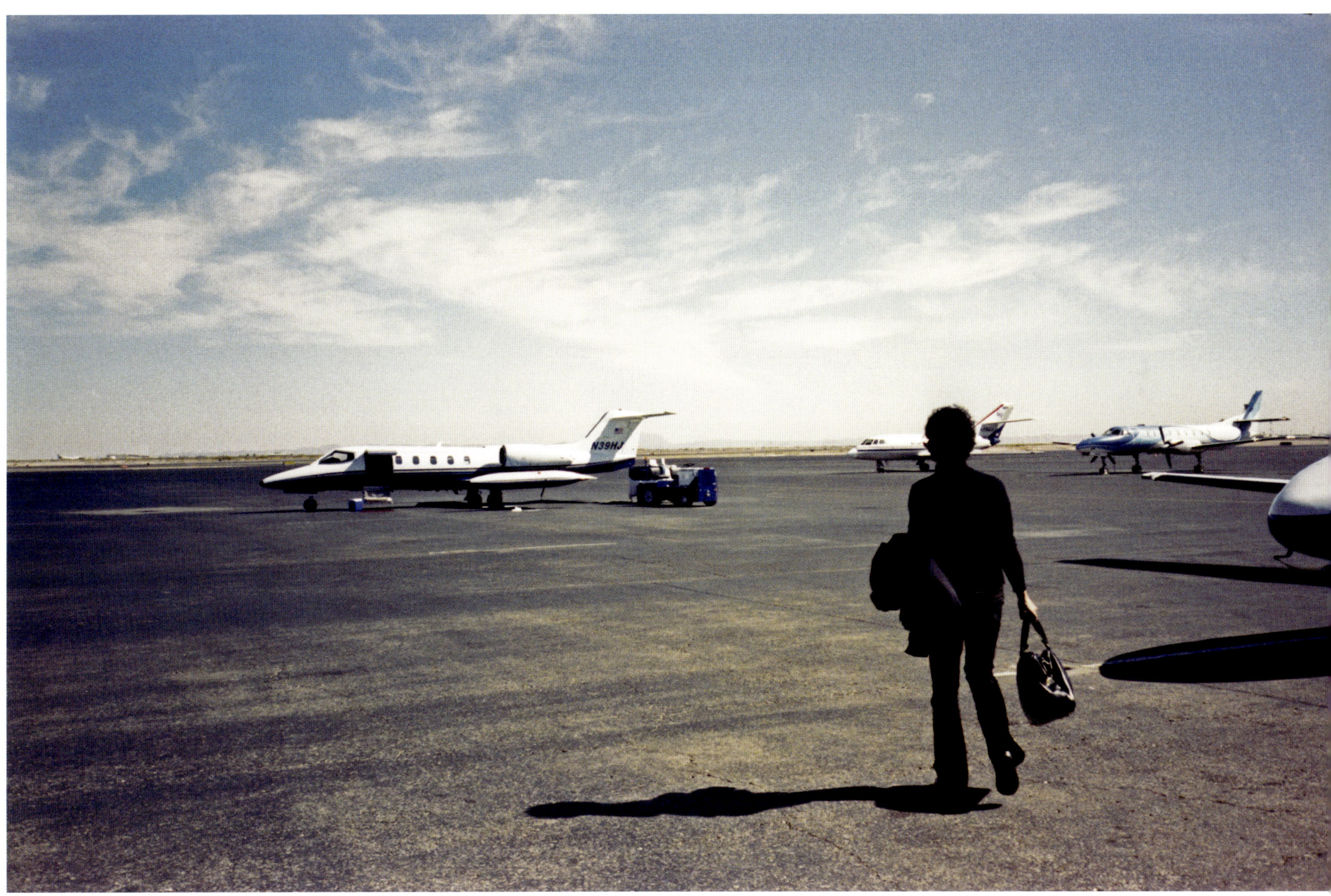
N39HJ

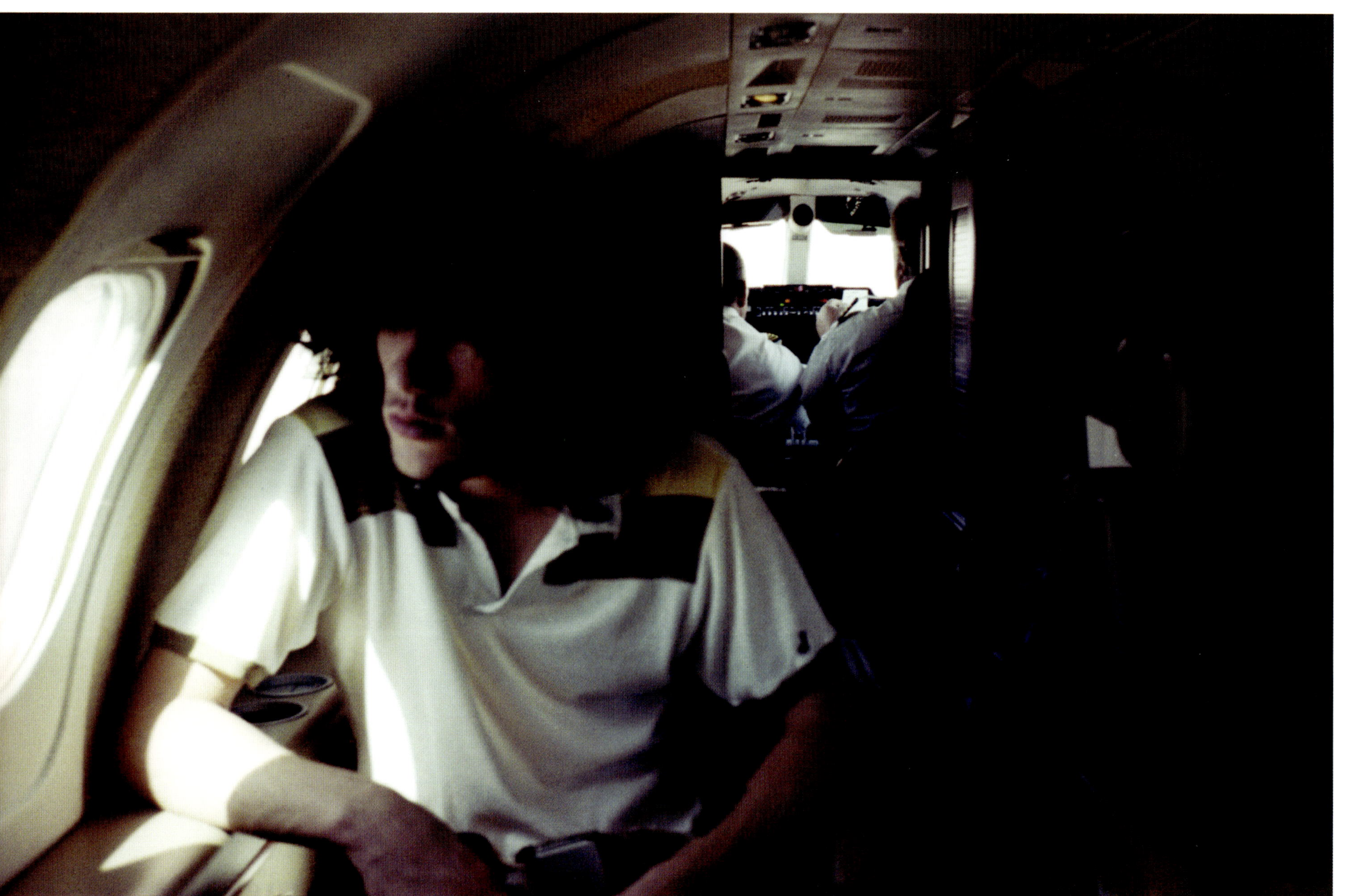

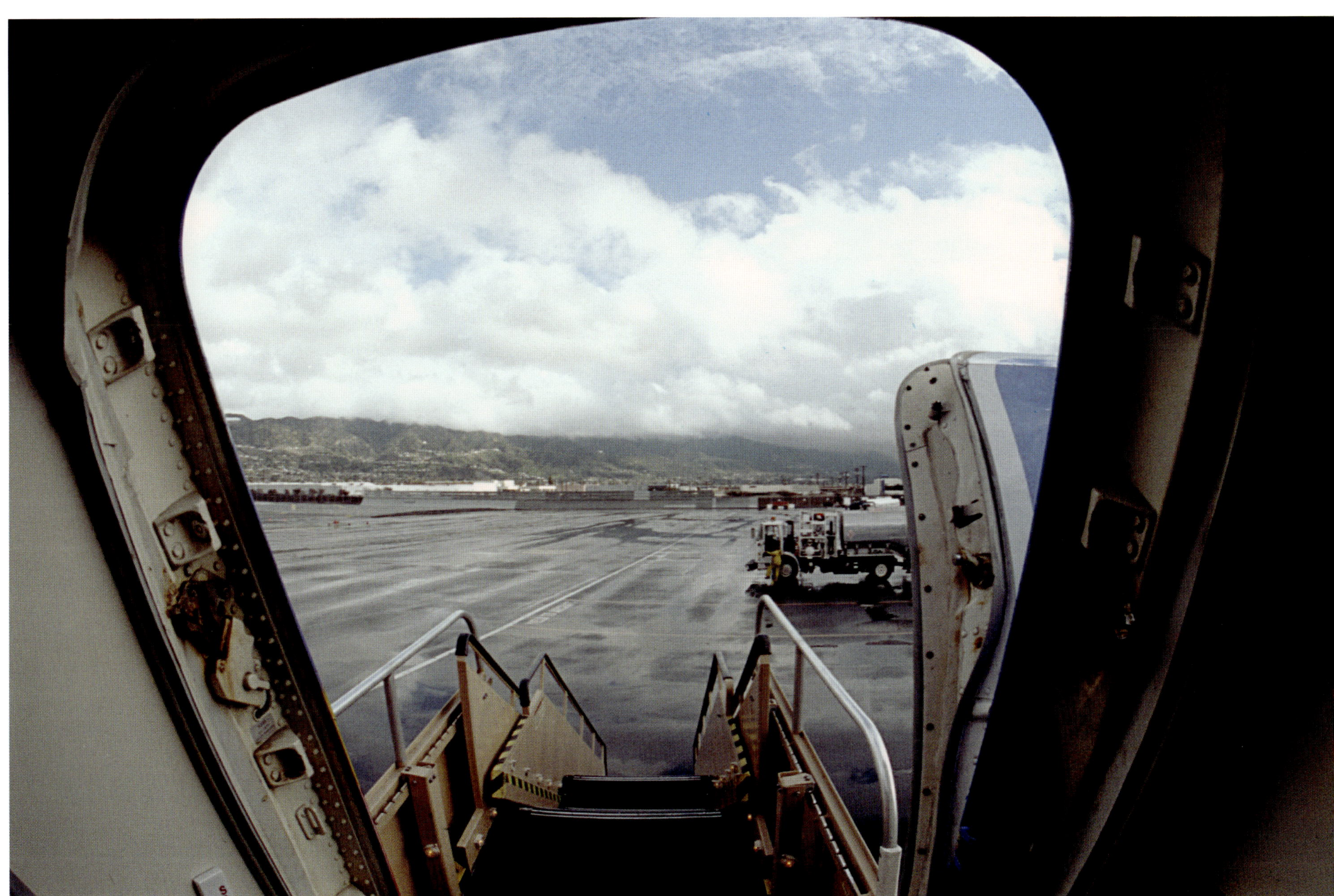

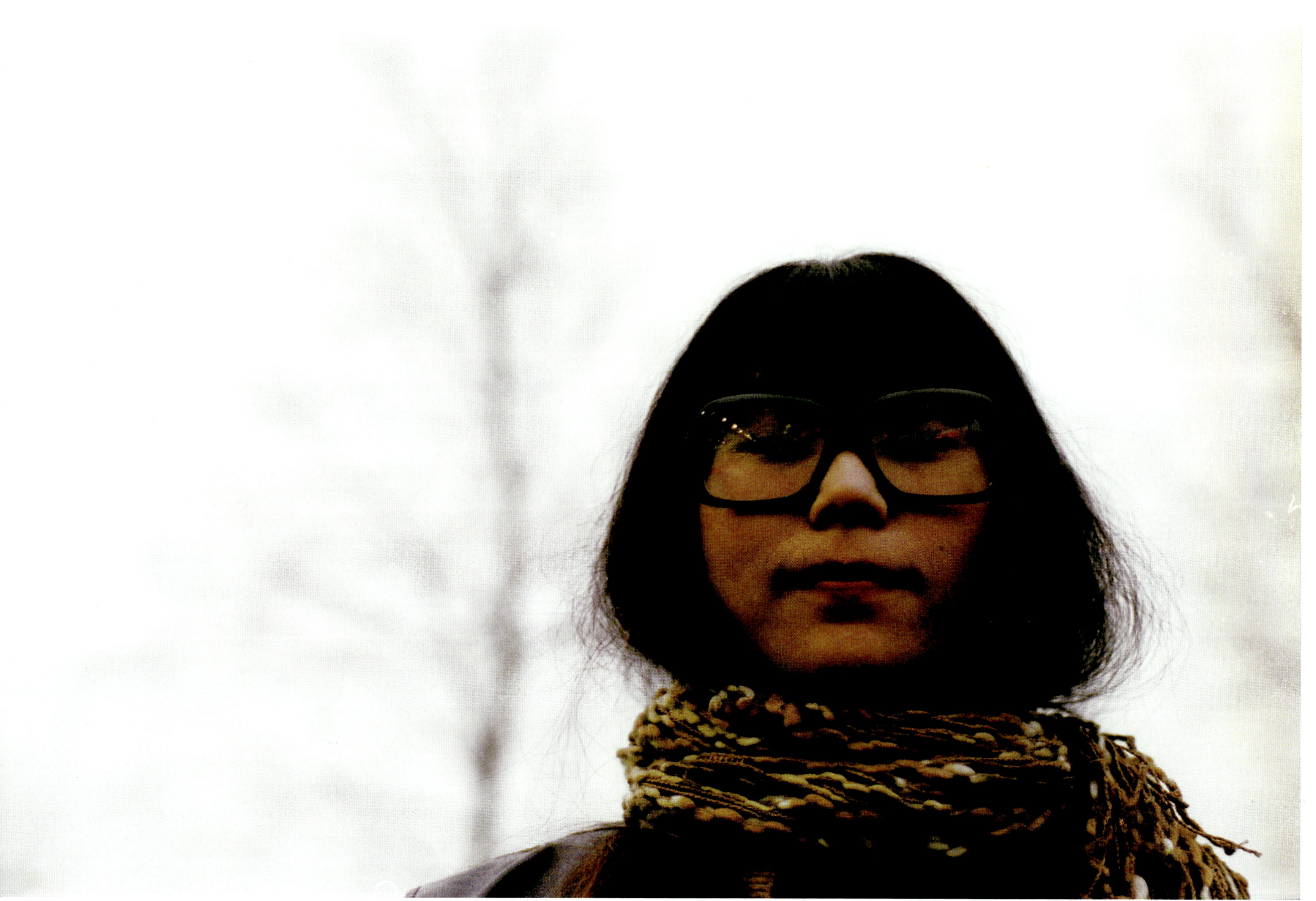

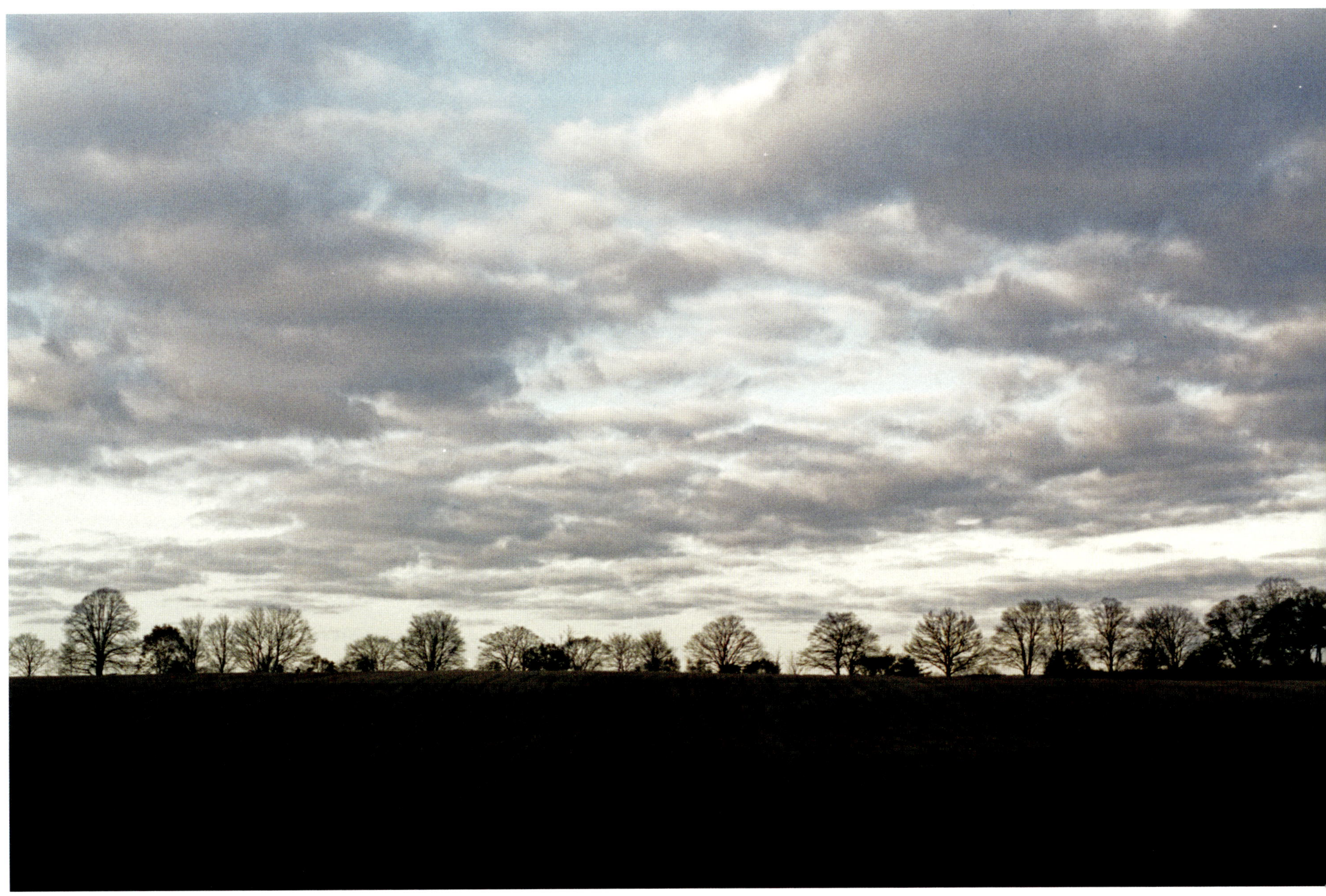

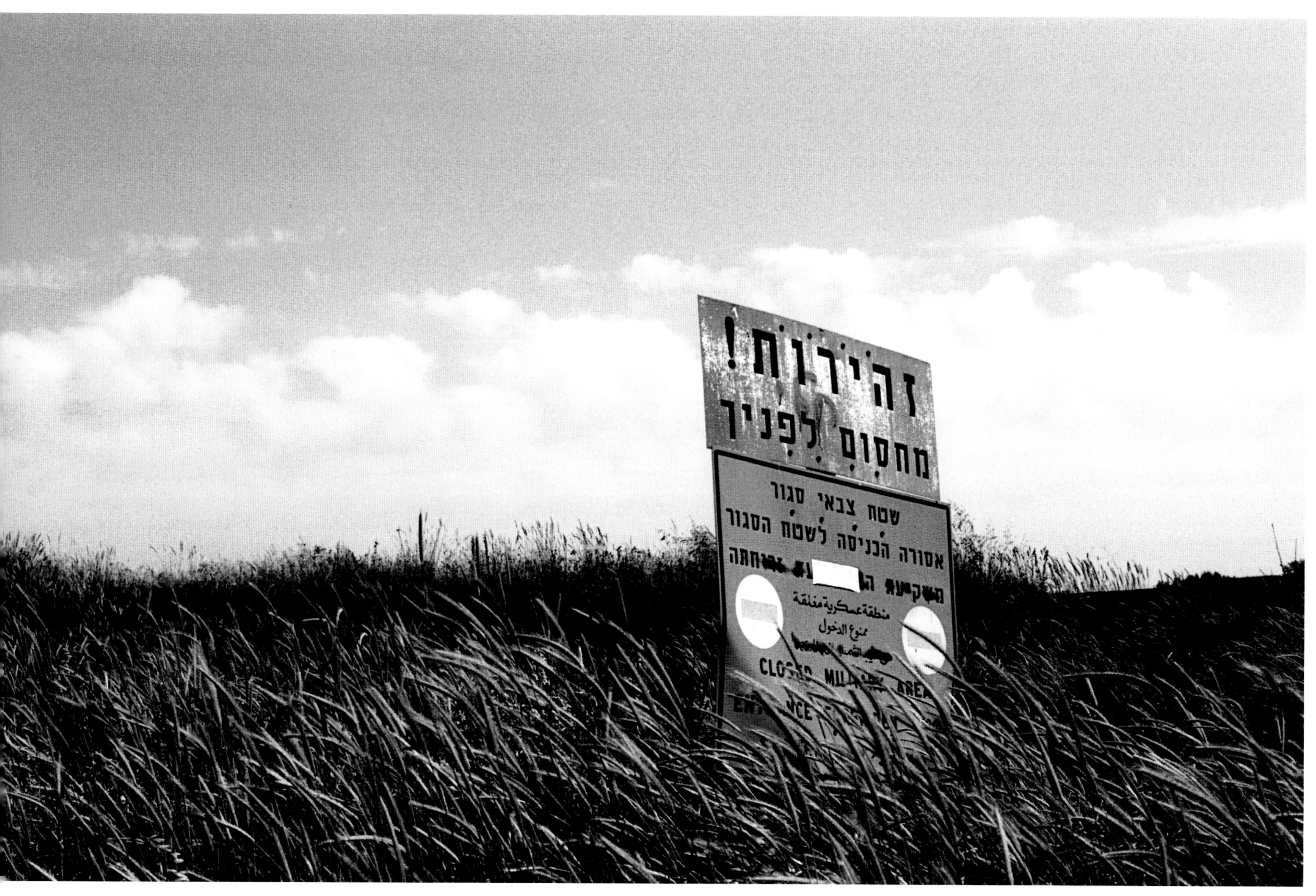
זהירות!
מחסום לפניך
שטח צבאי סגור
אסורה הכניסה לשטח הסגור
منطقة عسكرية مغلقة
ممنوع الدخول

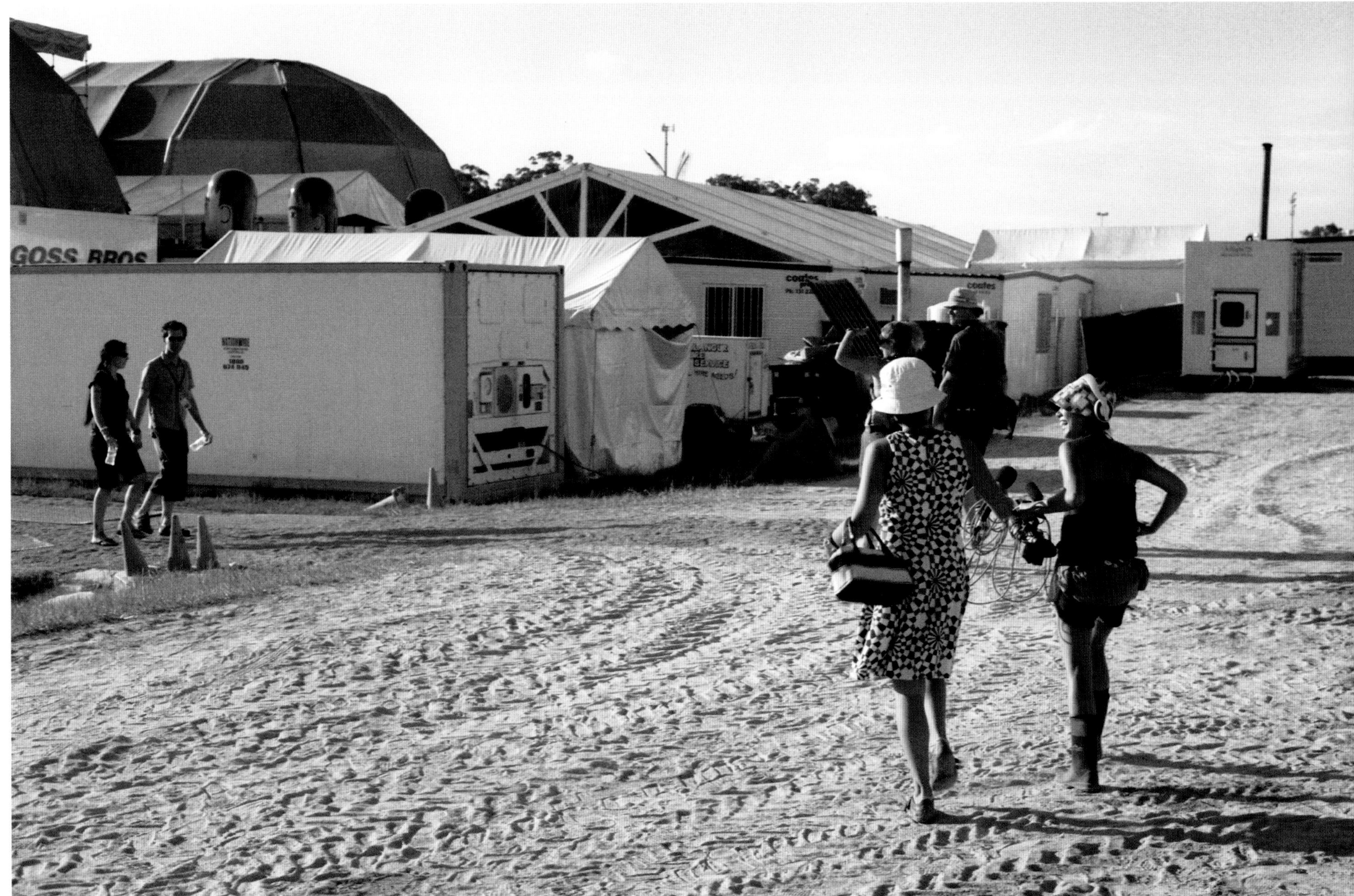
GOSS BROS
coates
coates

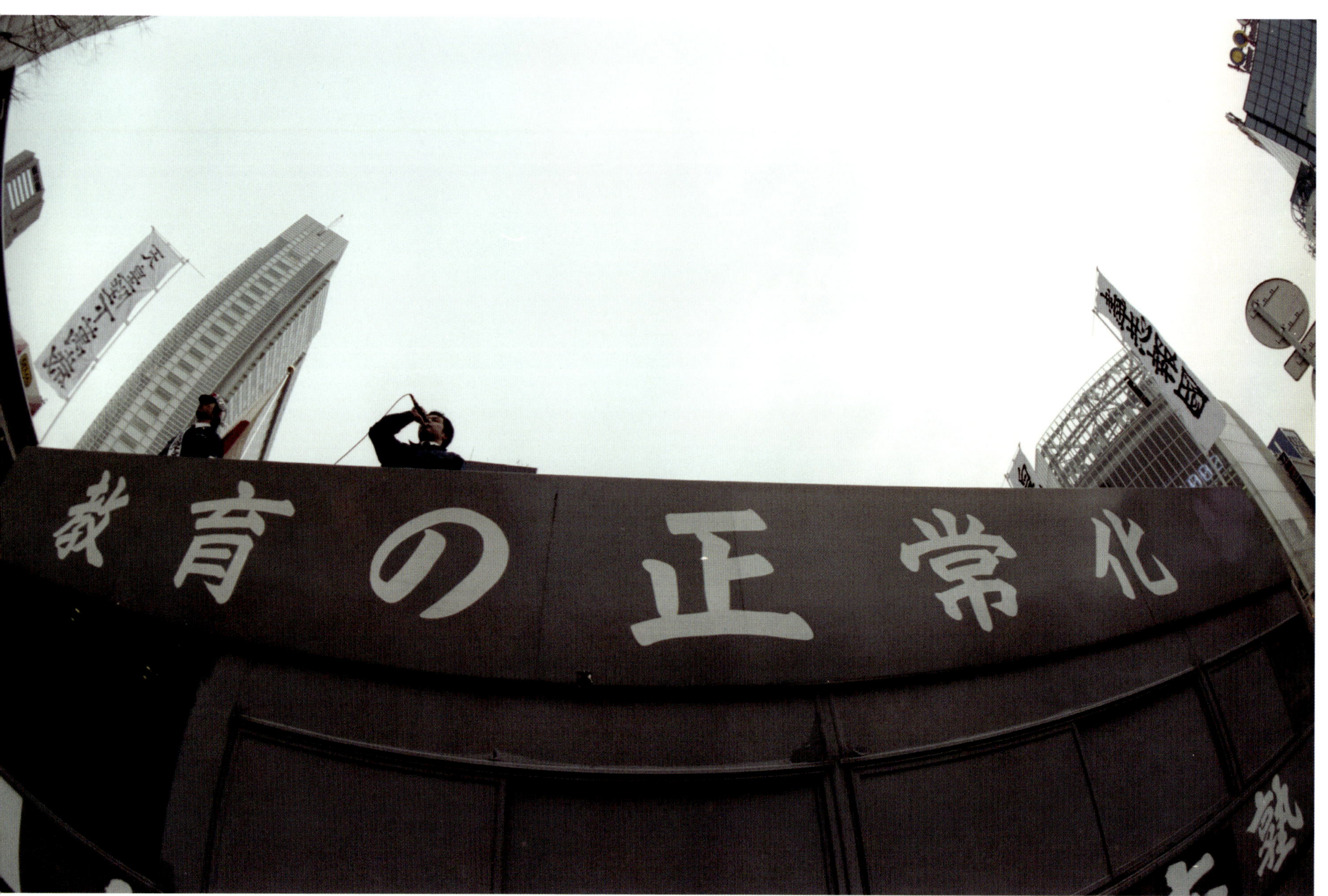
教育の正常化

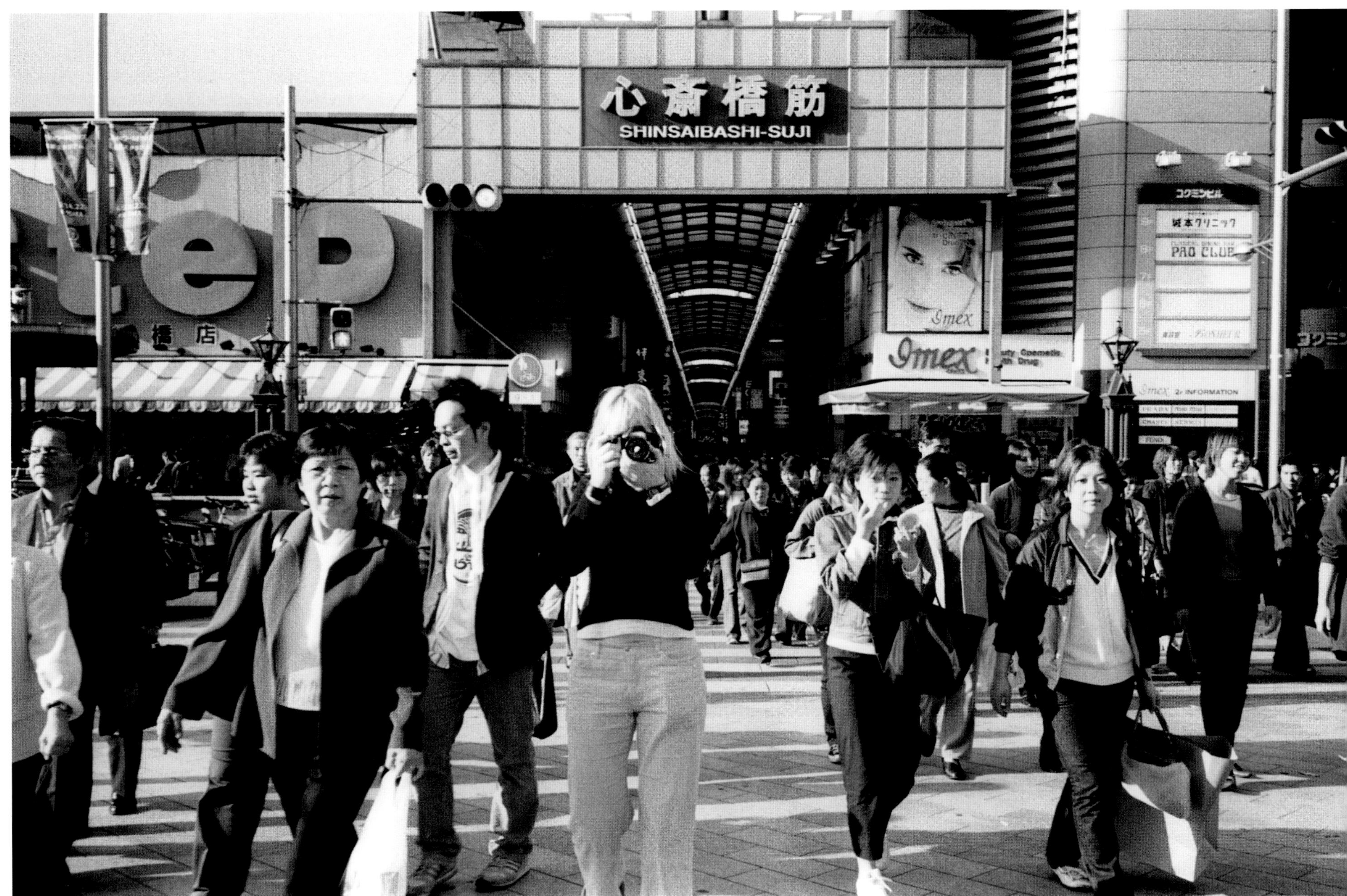

心斎橋筋
SHINSAIBASHI-SUJI
Imex
PAO CLUB

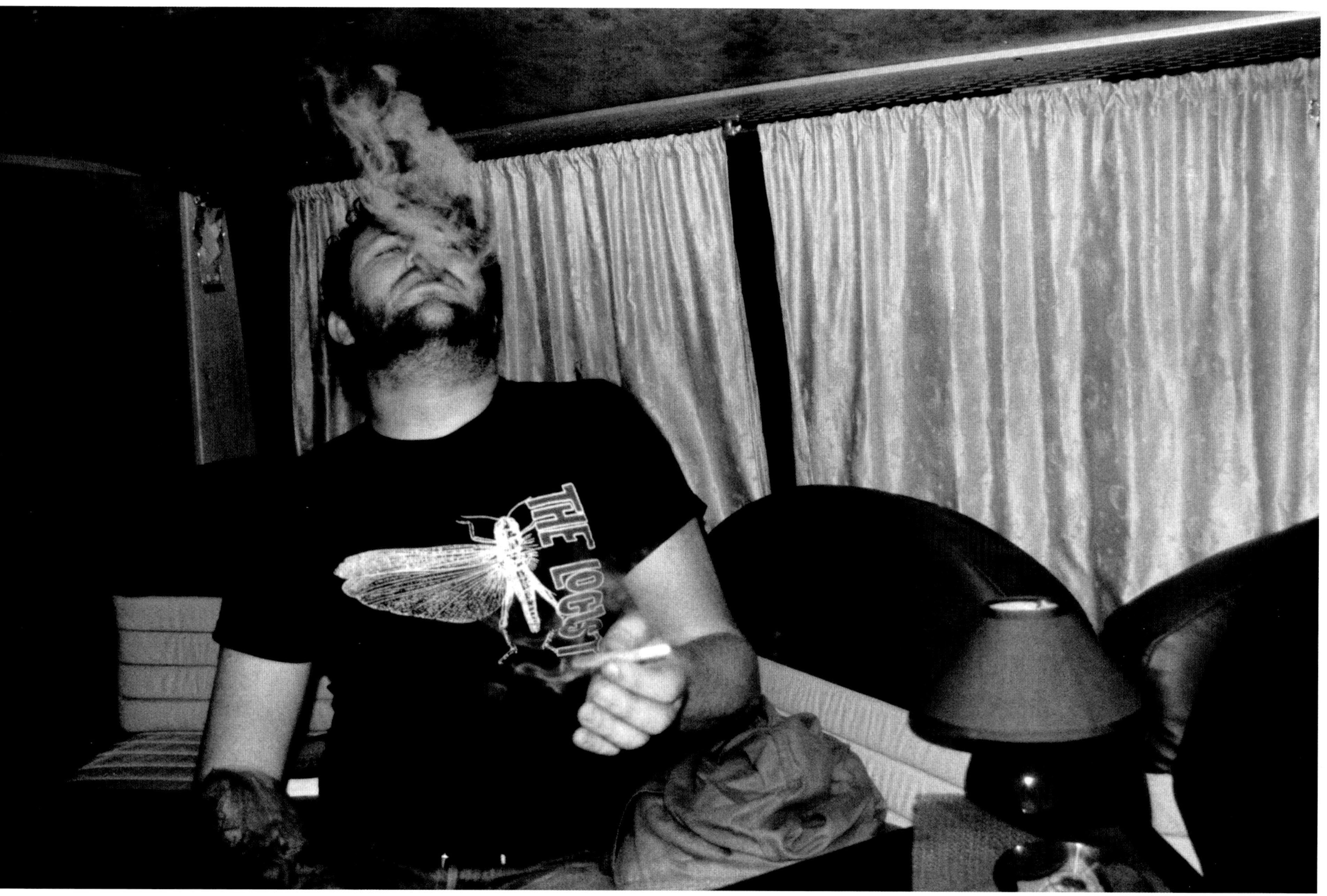
THE LOCUST

UNIVERSAL
Dear Cedric and
Omar –
Welcome to Holland. Here's a little present
for you, enjoy! Best wishes,
Universal Holland
WITH COMPLIMENTS
UNIVERSAL MUSIC
UNIVERSAL MUSIC B.V.
ENLAAN 4, P.O. BOX 23, 3740 AA BAARN, THE NETHERLANDS. TEL (31) 35 626 1500
www.universalmusic.nl
KING SIZE
Smoking
BLUE
KING SIZE
Smoking
BLUE

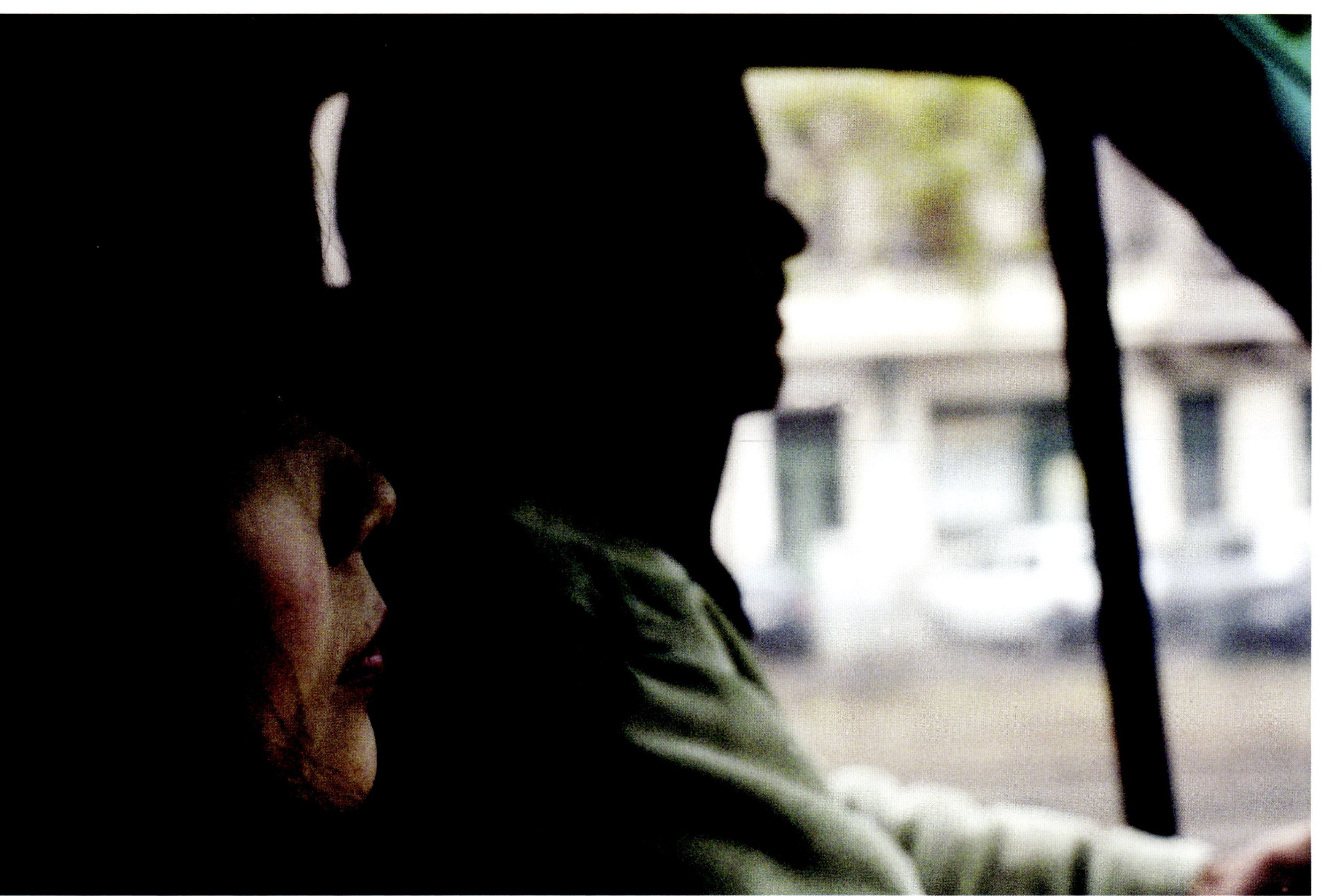

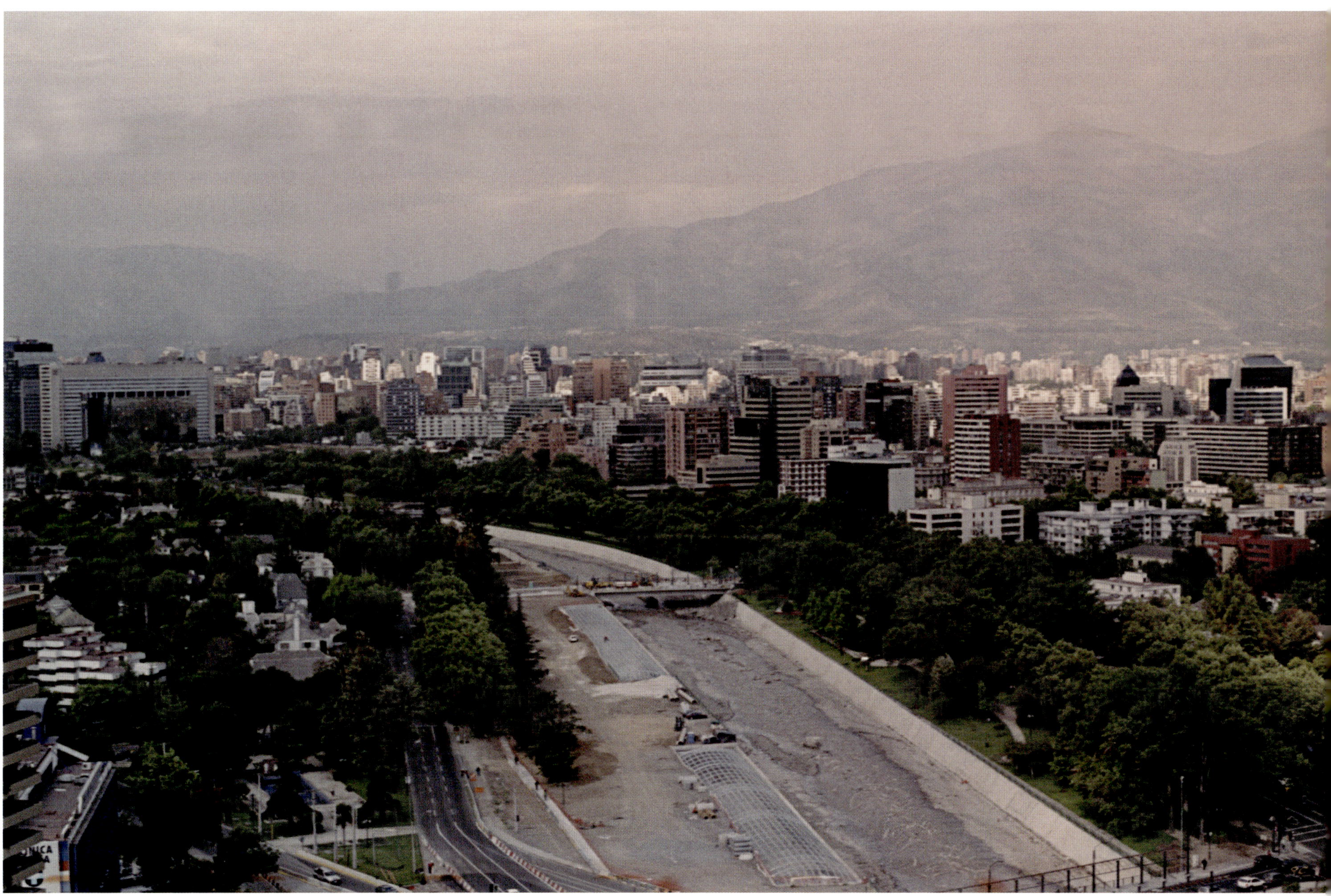

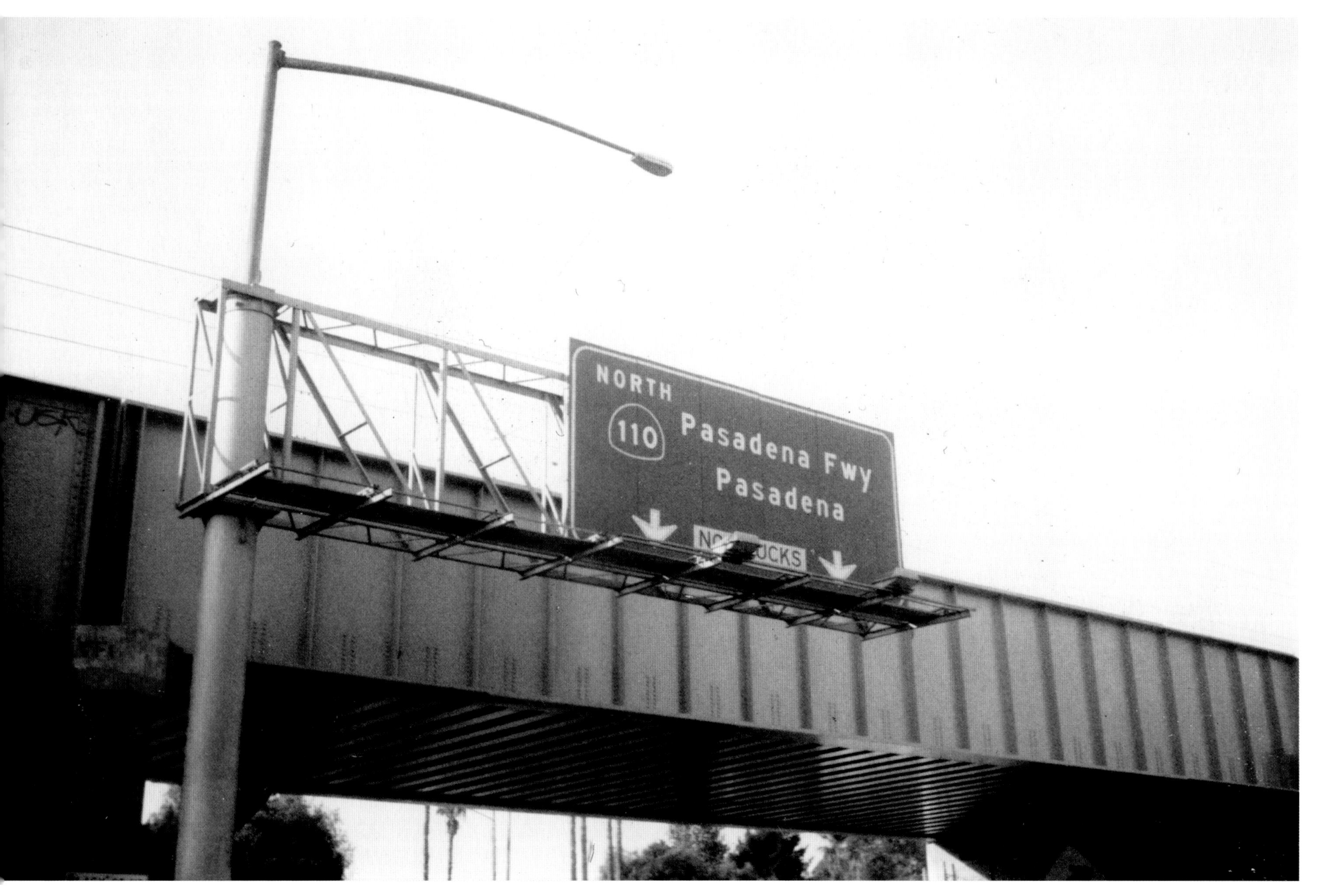
NORTH
110
Pasadena Fwy
Pasadena

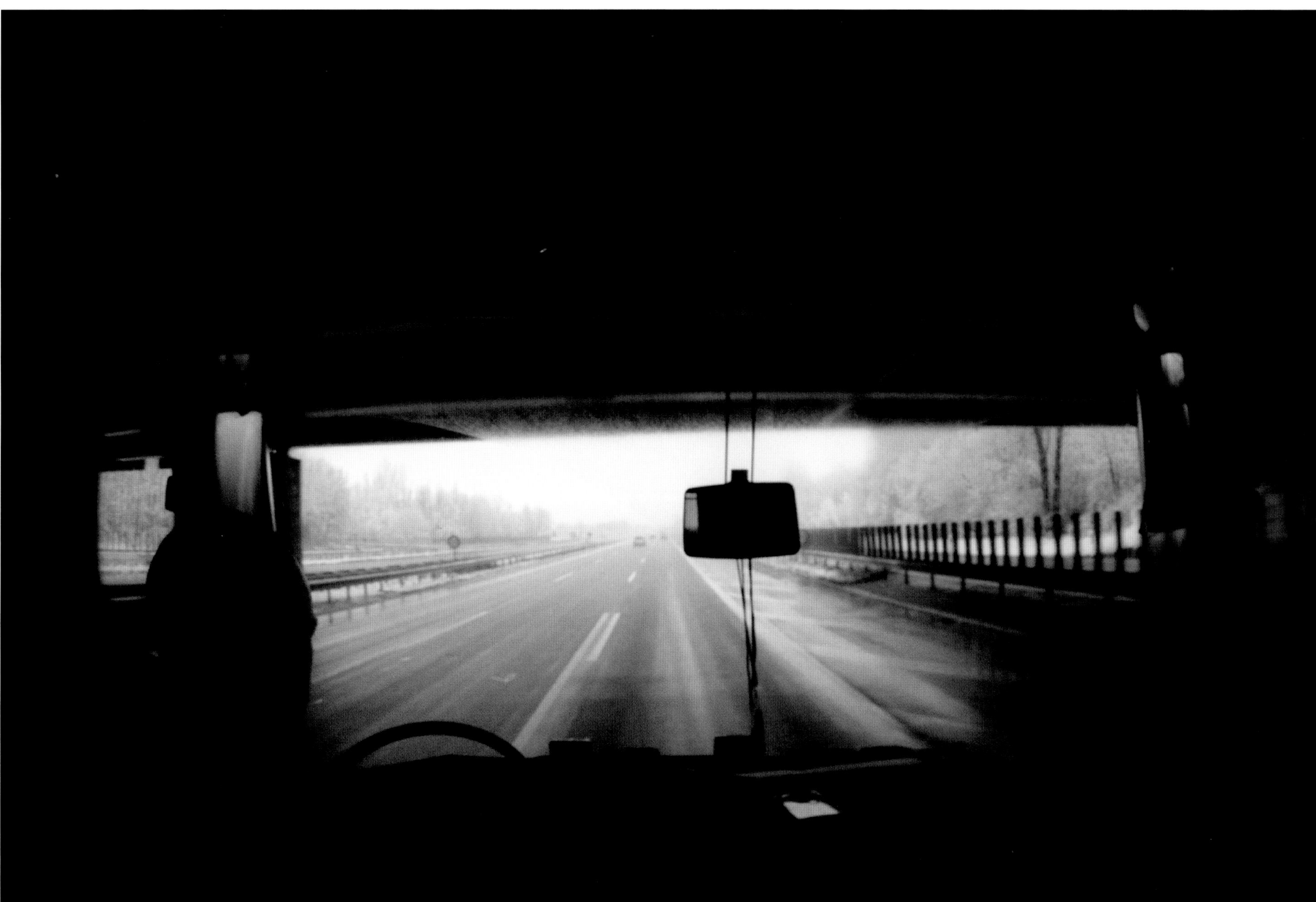

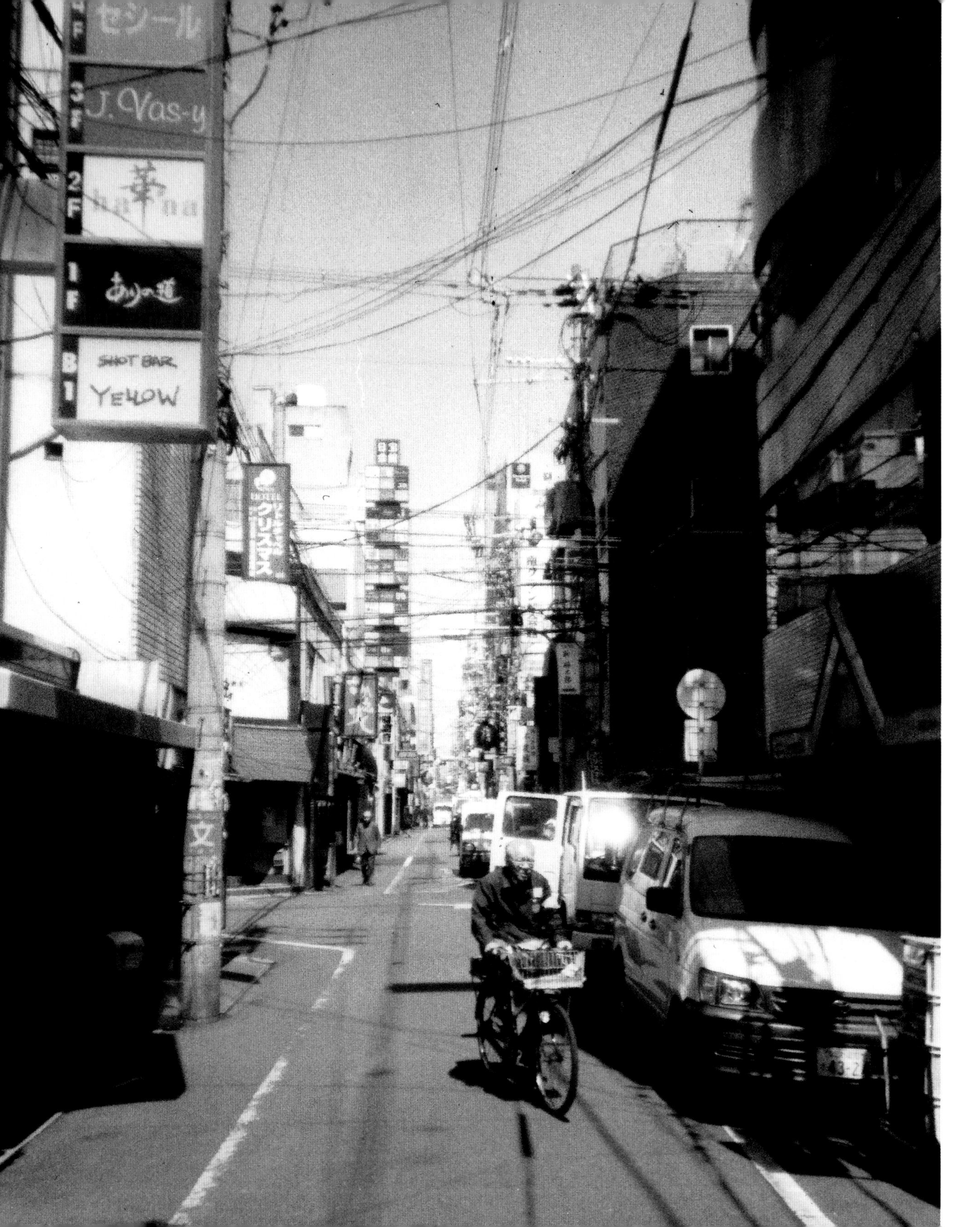
セシール
J. Vas-y
SHOT BAR
YELLOW
クリスマス

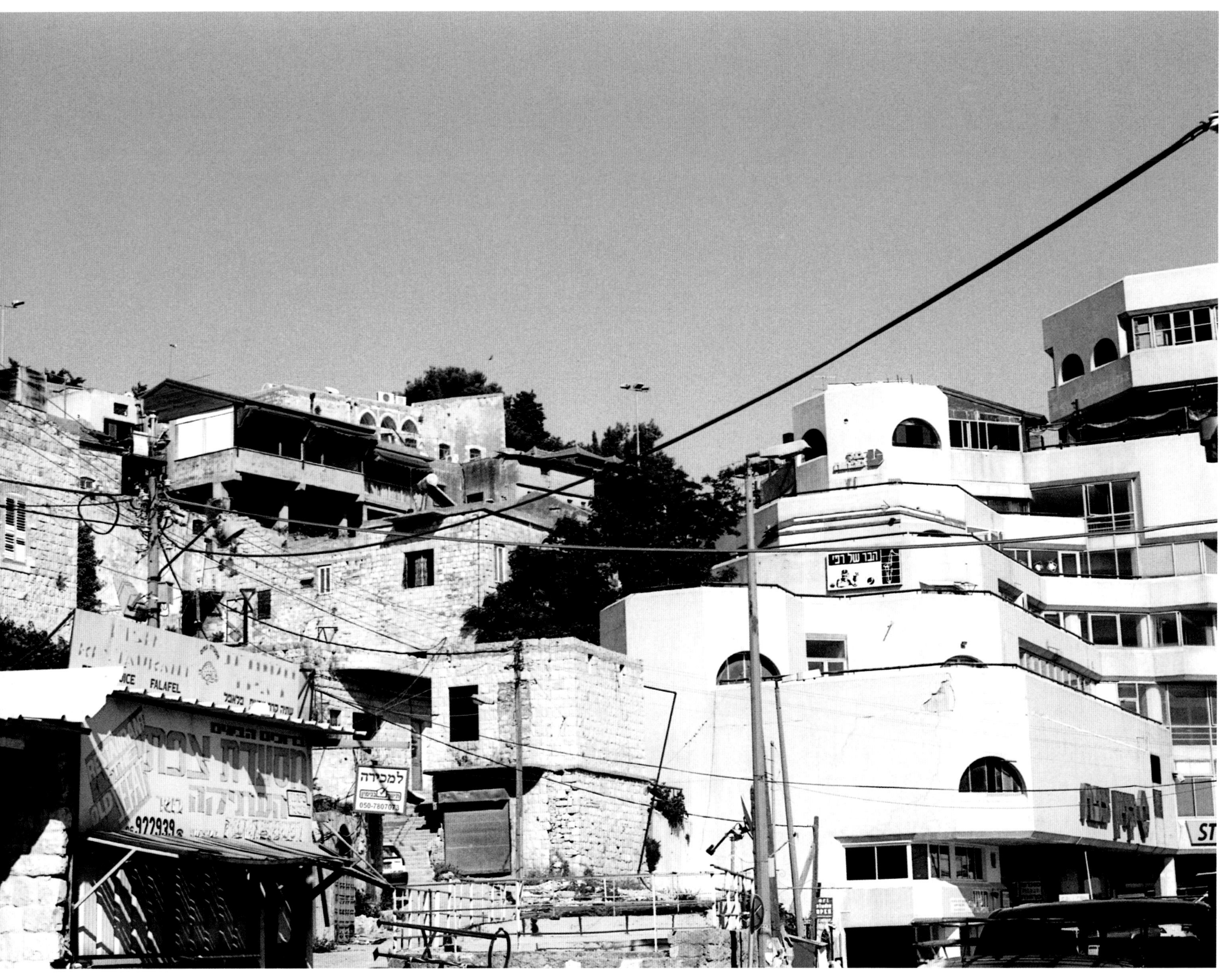
FALAFEL
למכירה
הבר של רפי

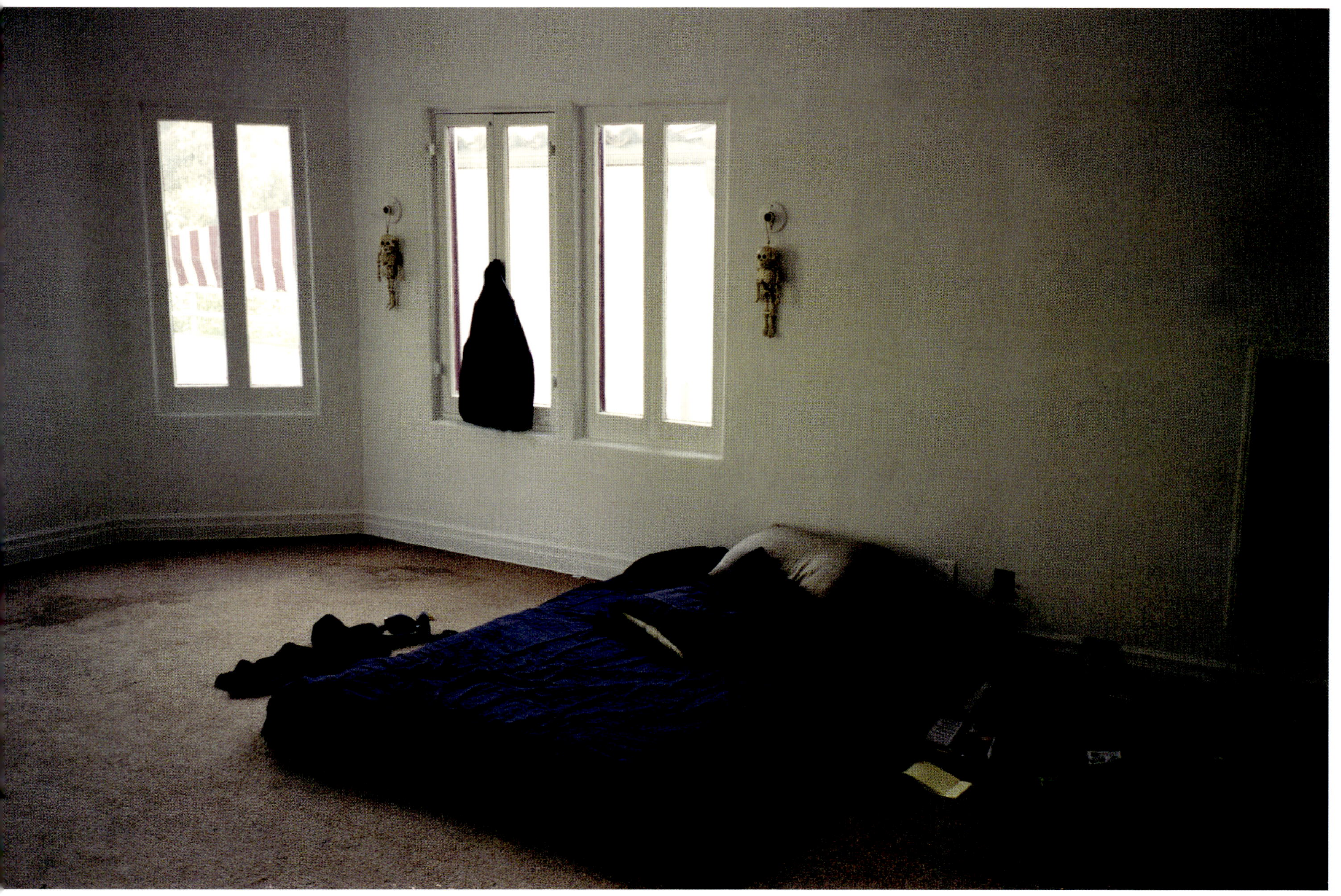

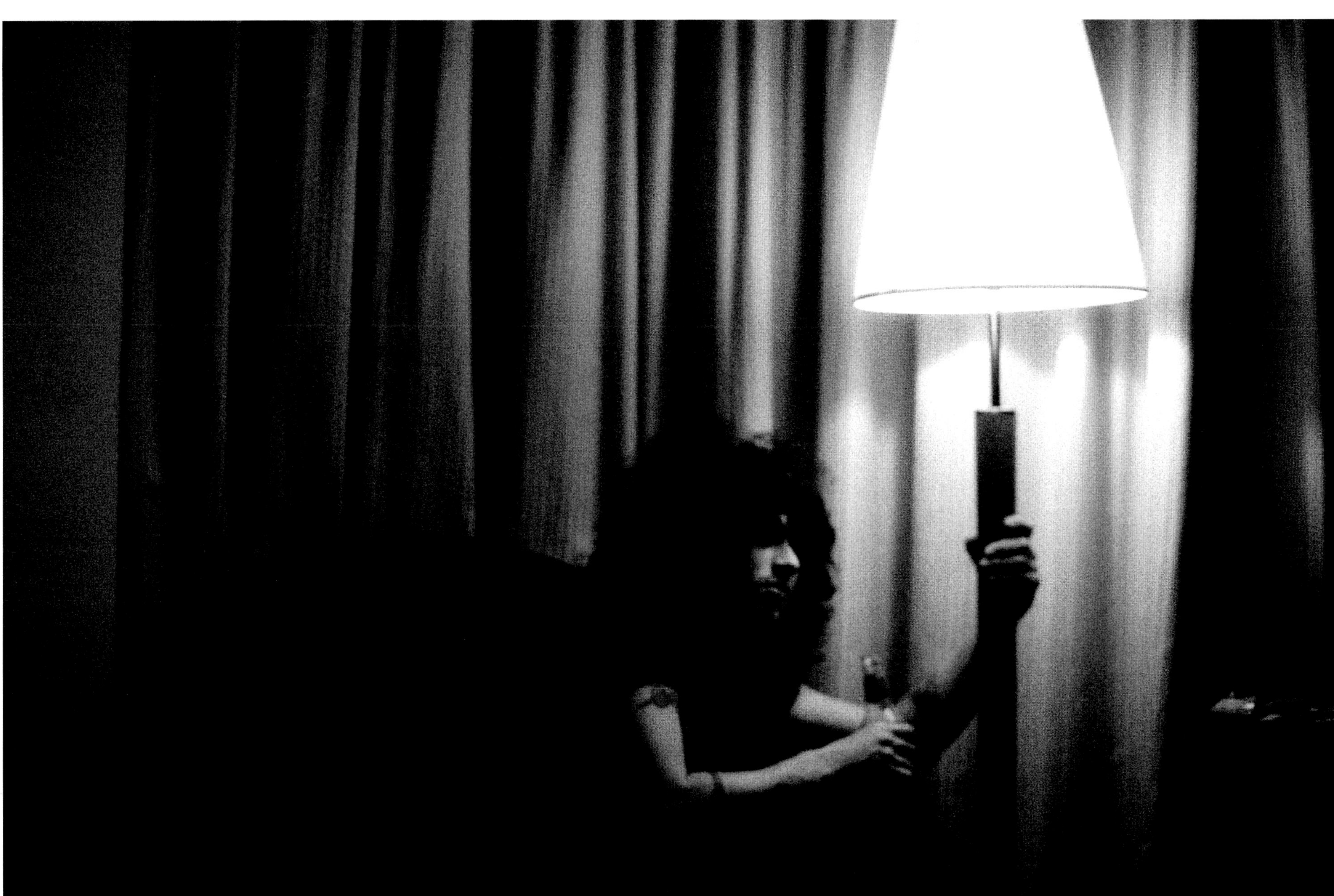

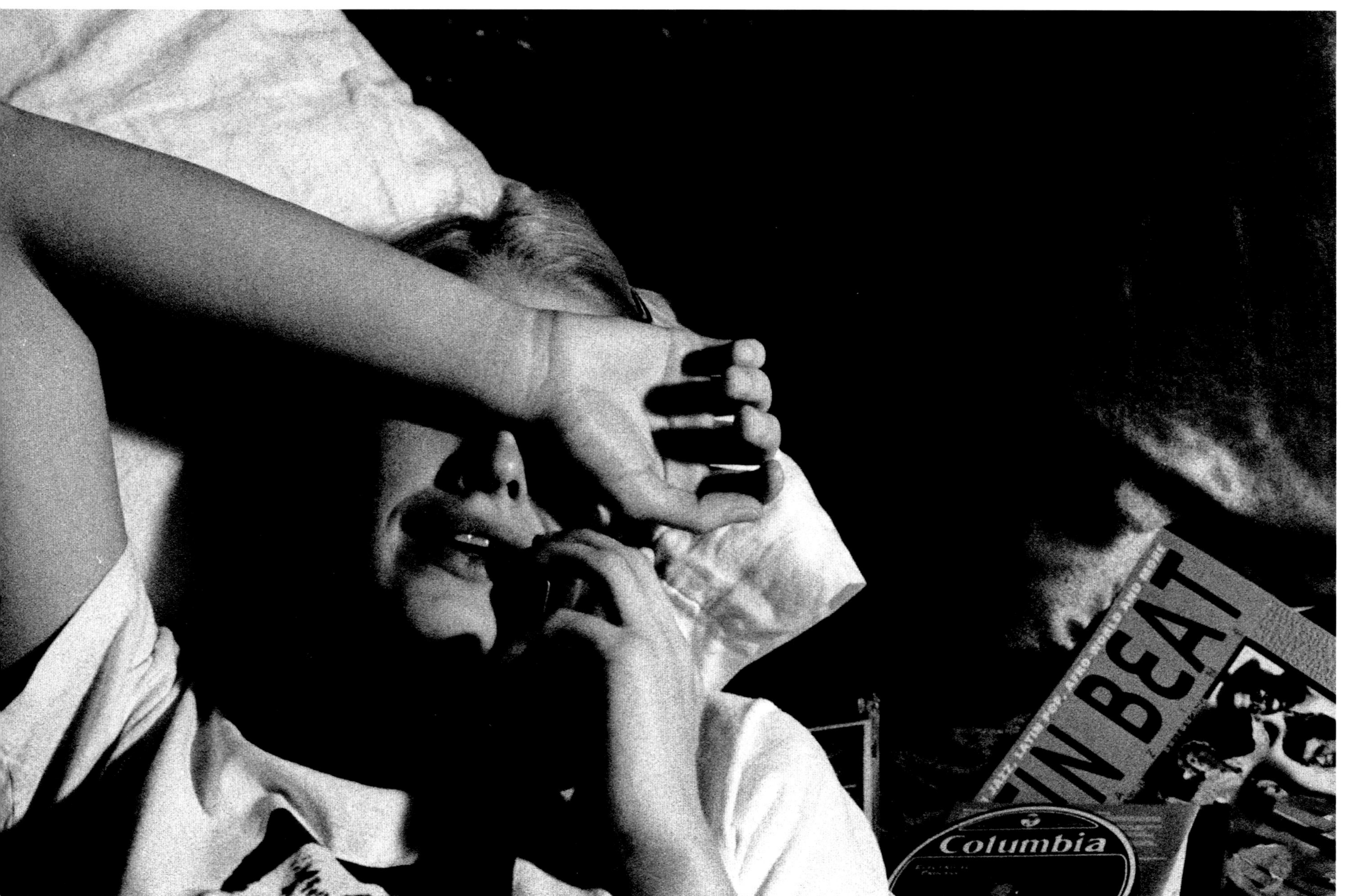

JAZZ, LATIN POP, AFRO-WORLD AND MORE
BEAT
Columbia

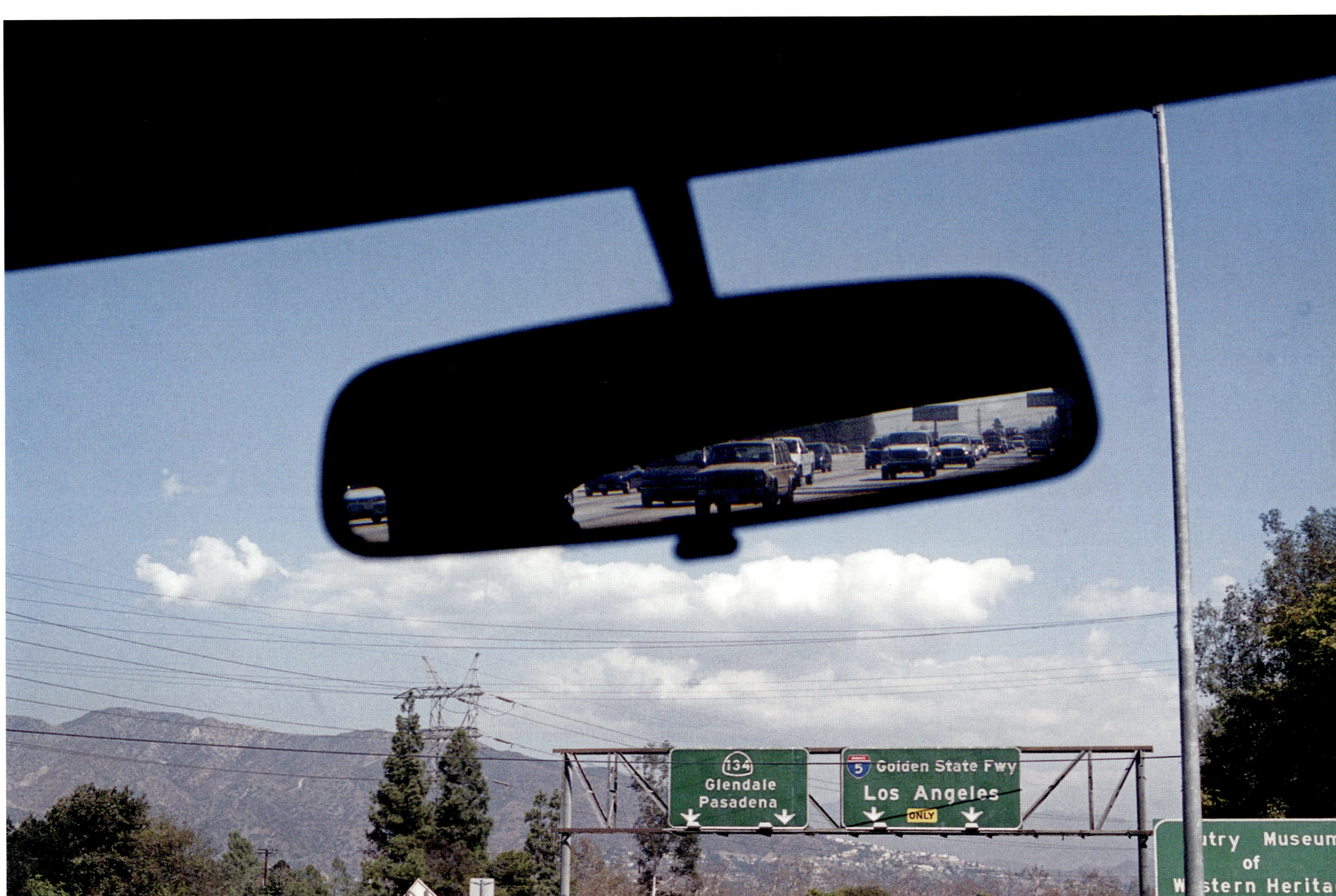
134
Glendale
Pasadena
5
Golden State Fwy
Los Angeles
ONLY
Museum
of

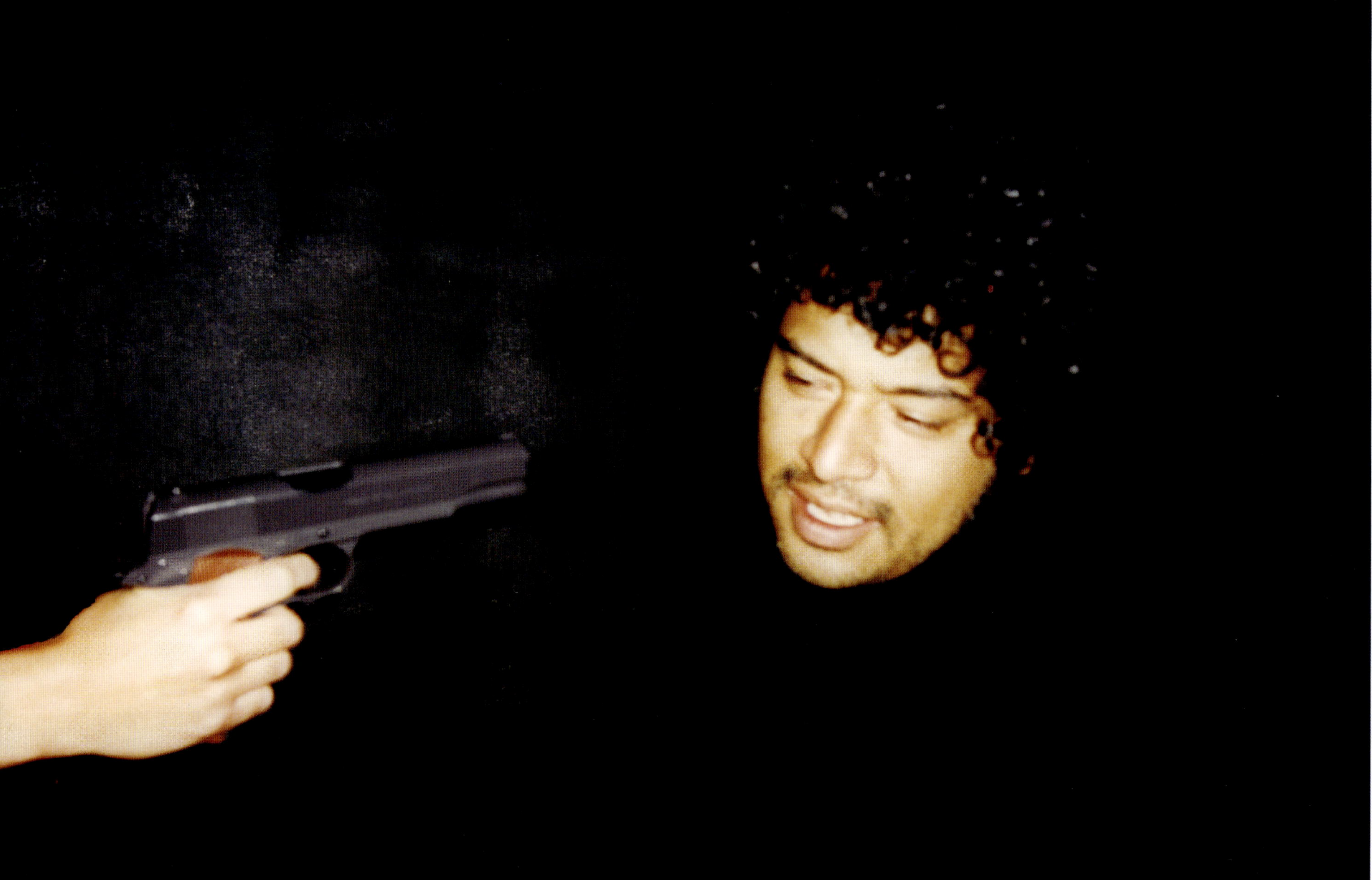

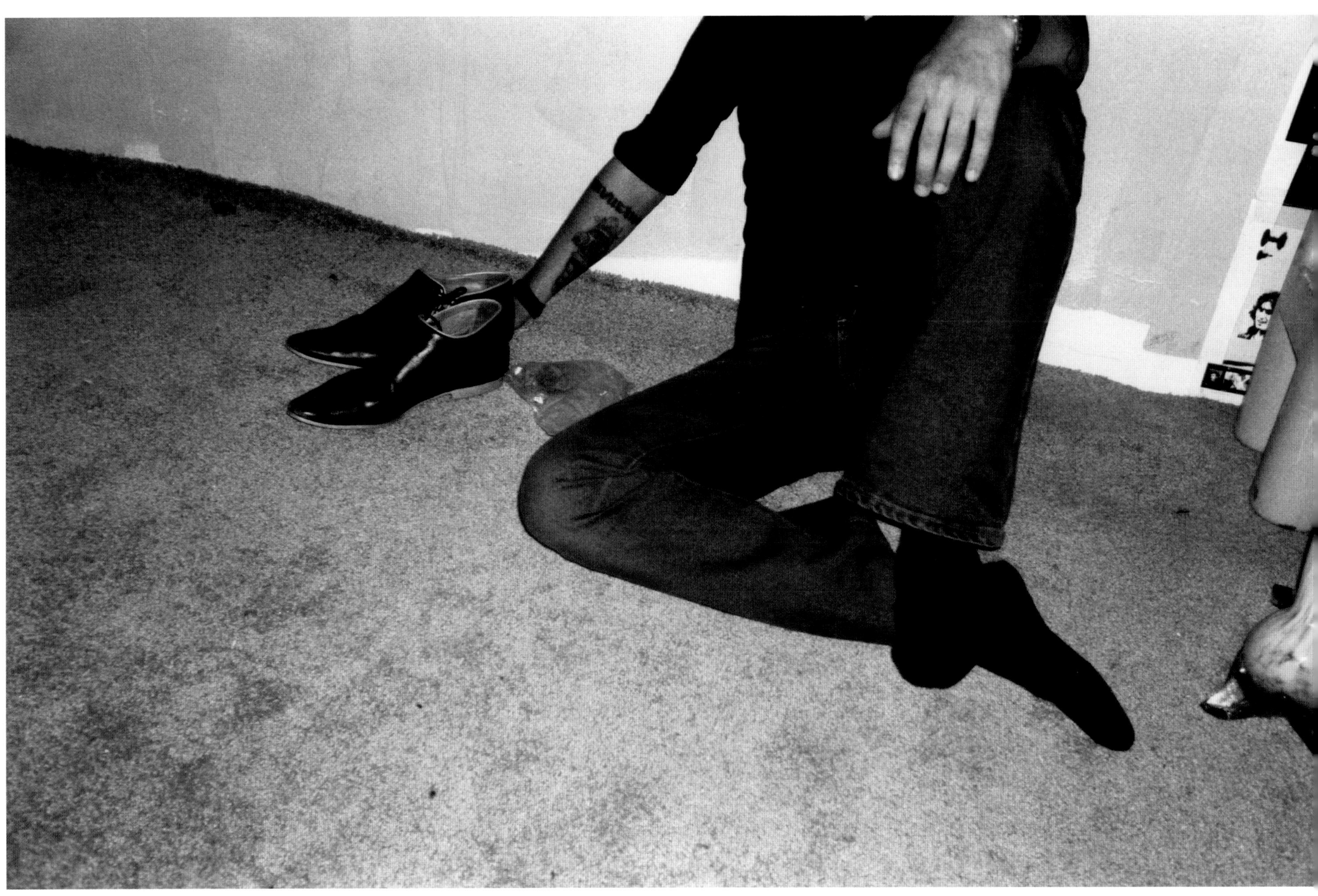

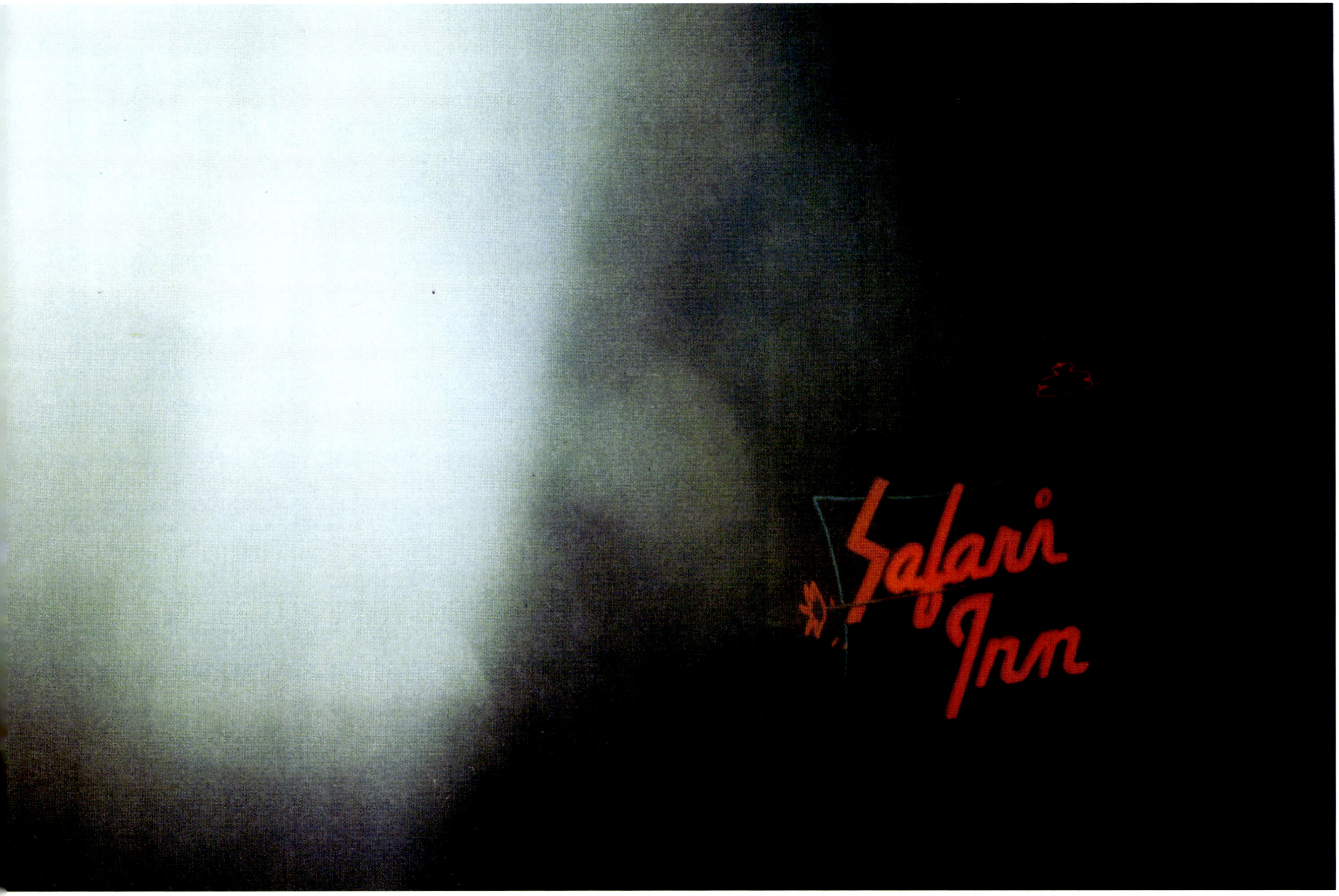

Safari
Inn

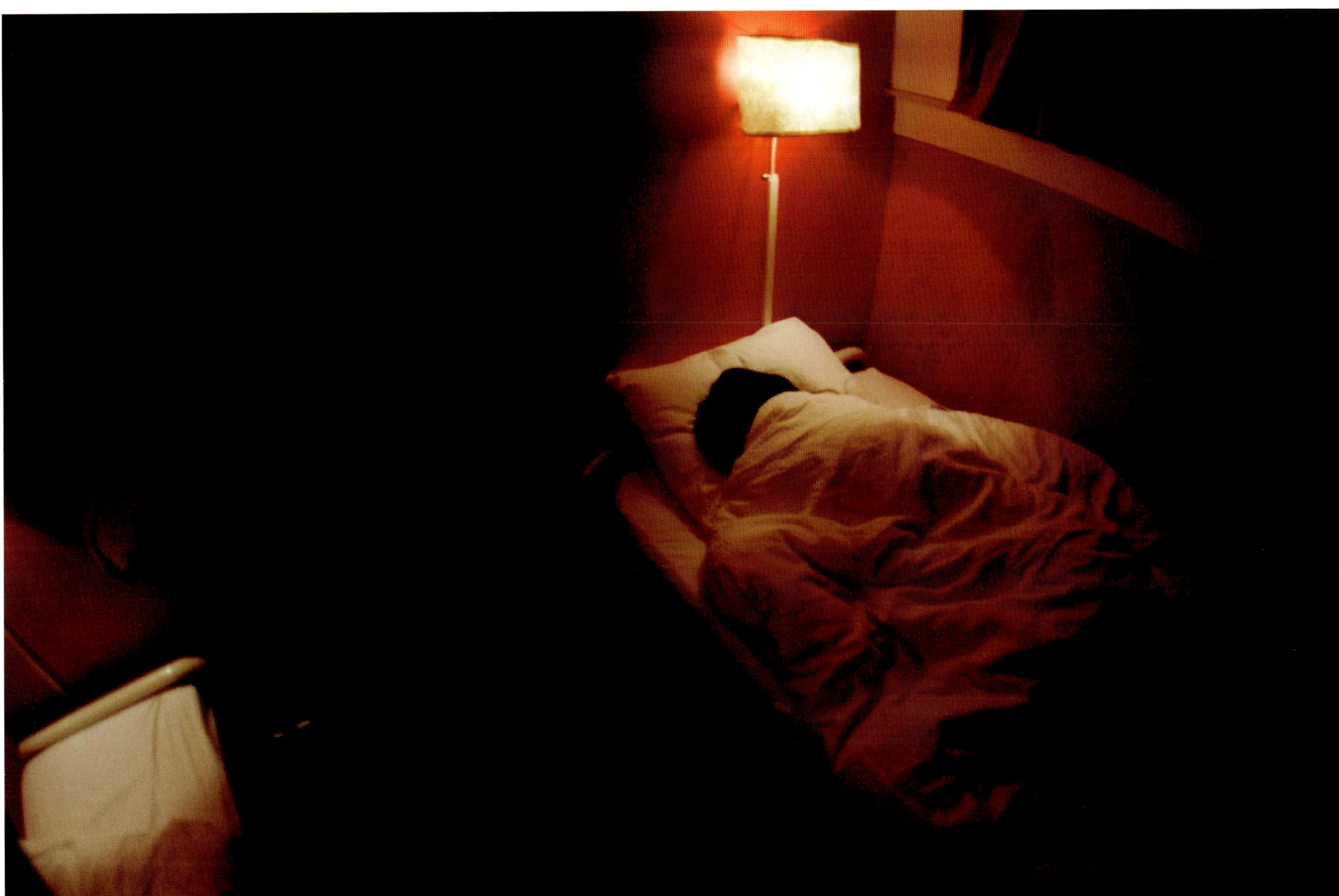

arderobe

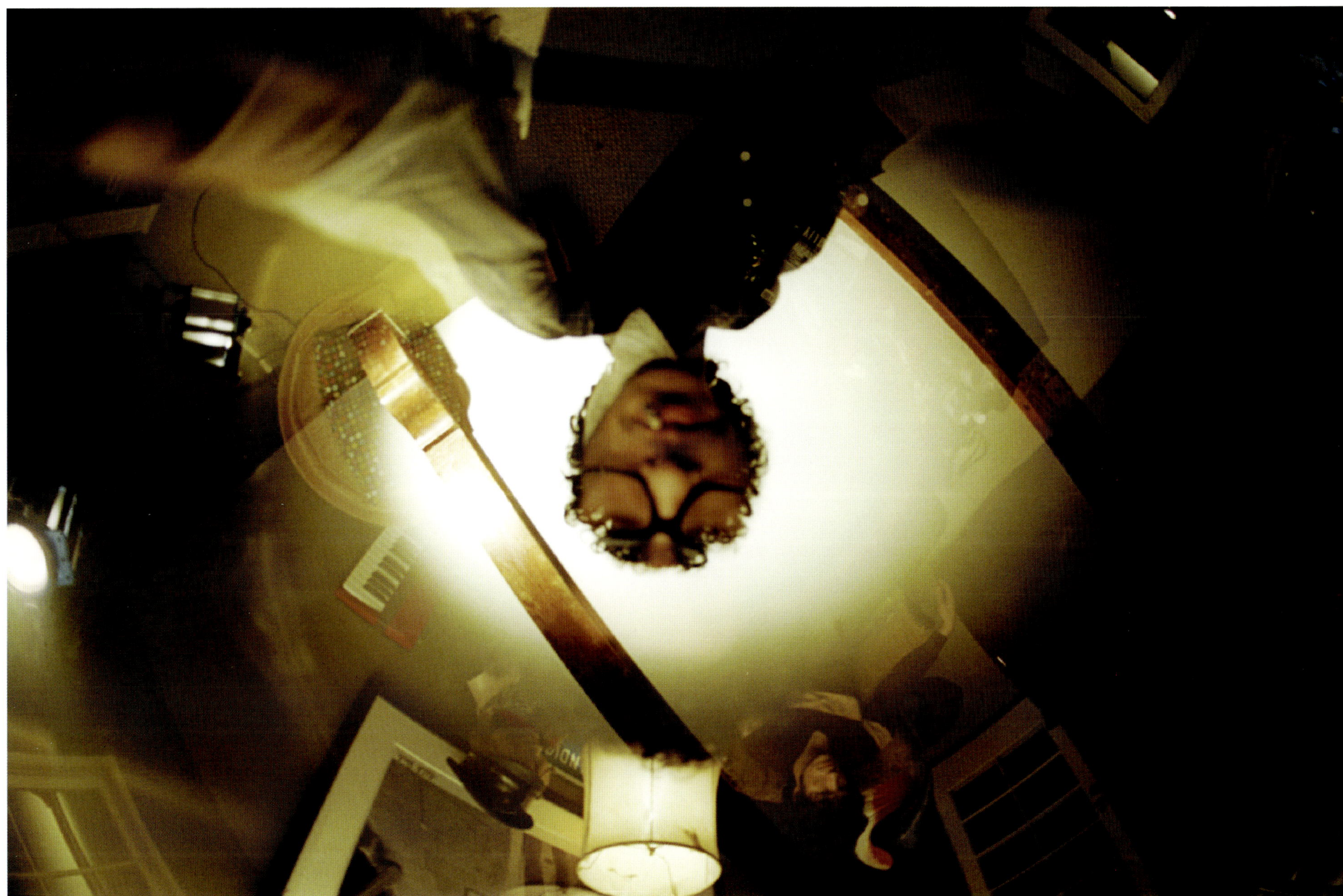

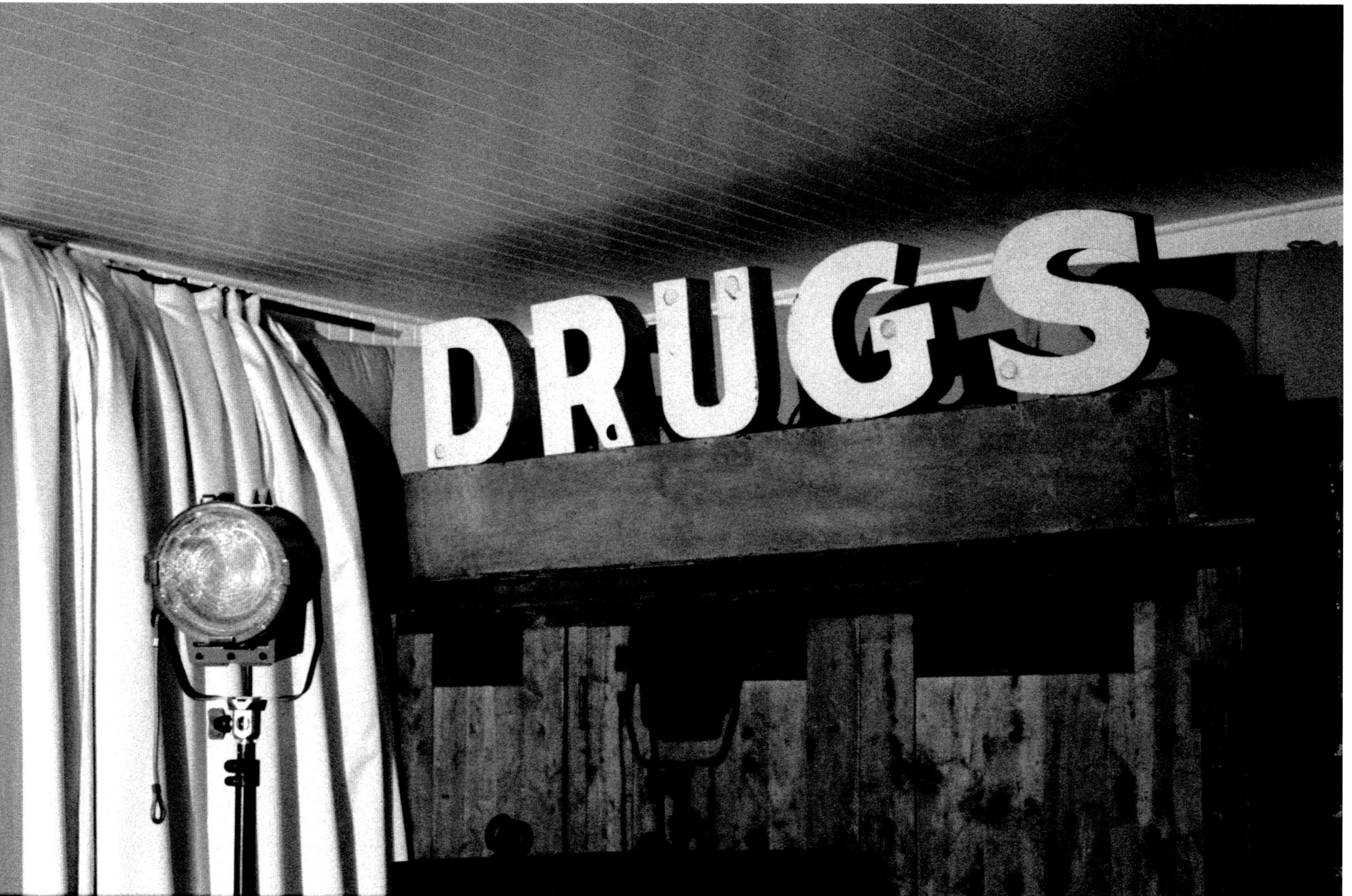
DRUGS

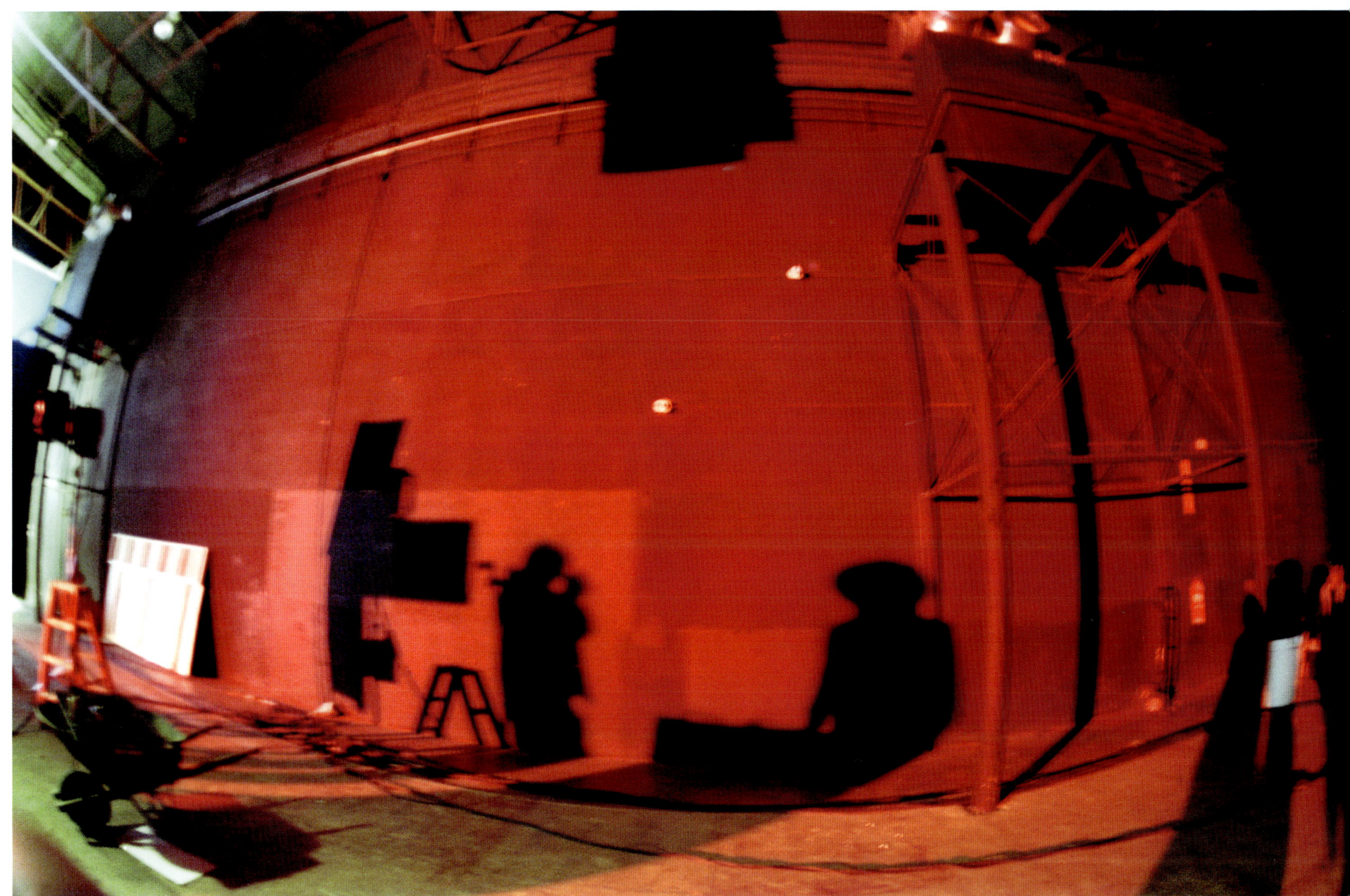

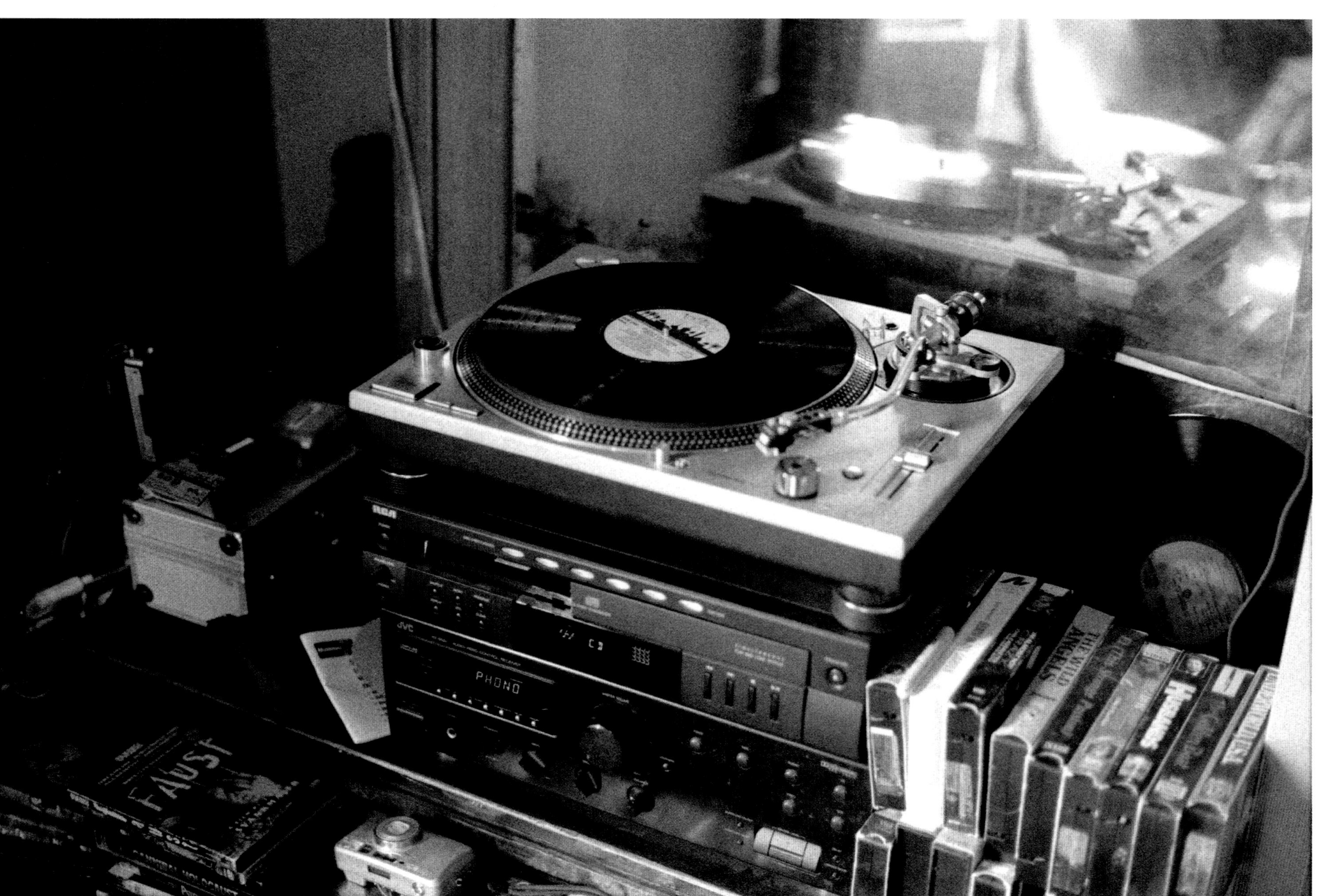
JVC
PHONO
THE WILD ANGELS
FAUST

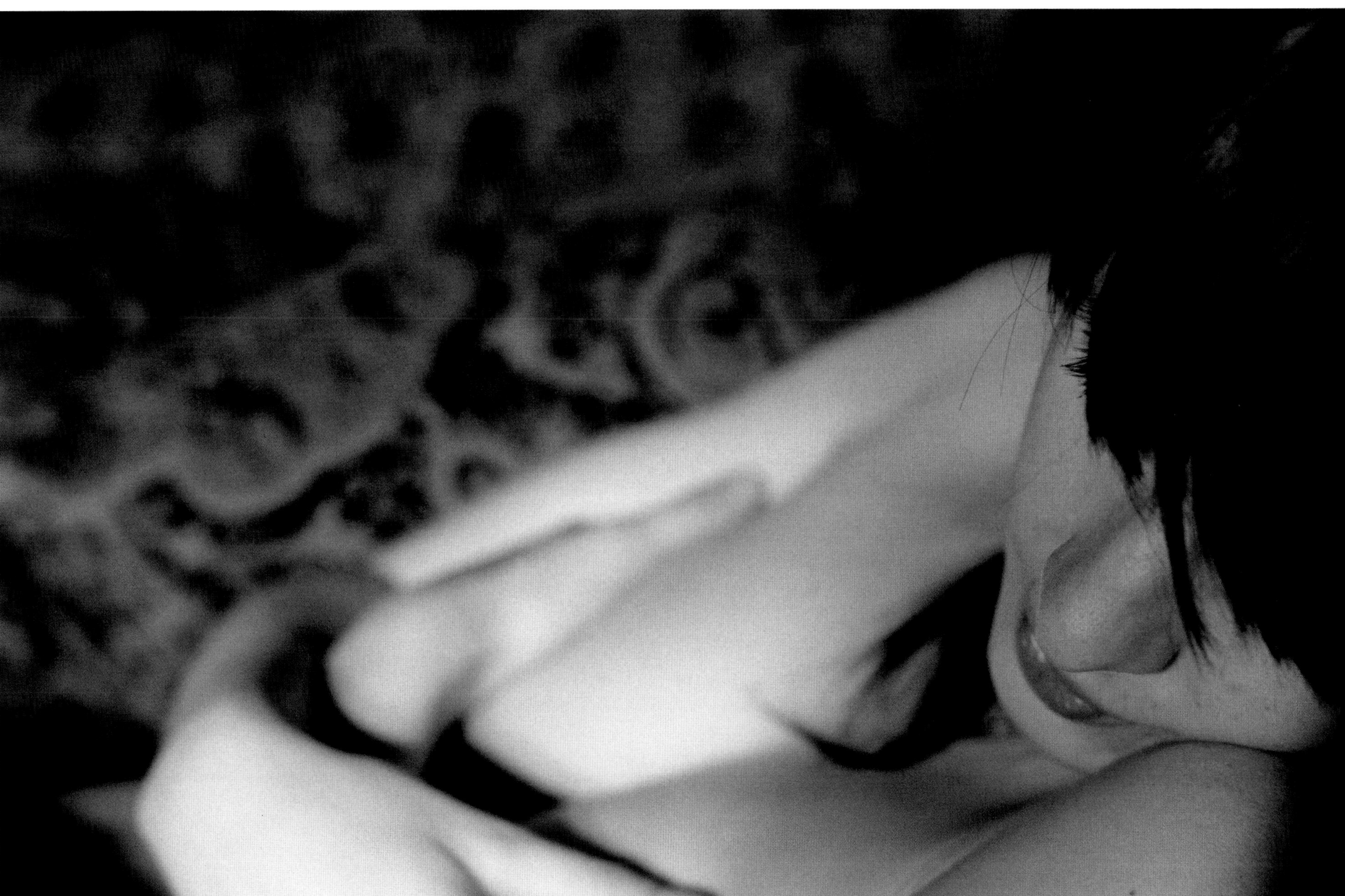

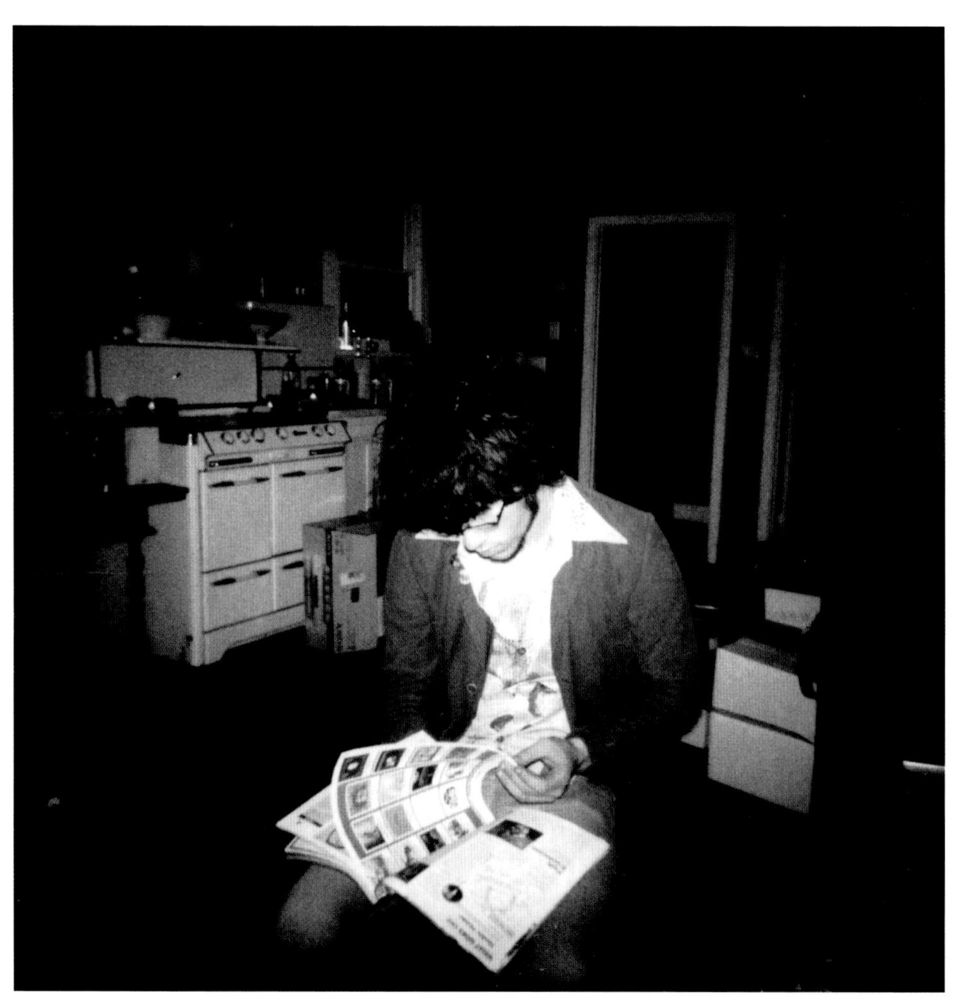

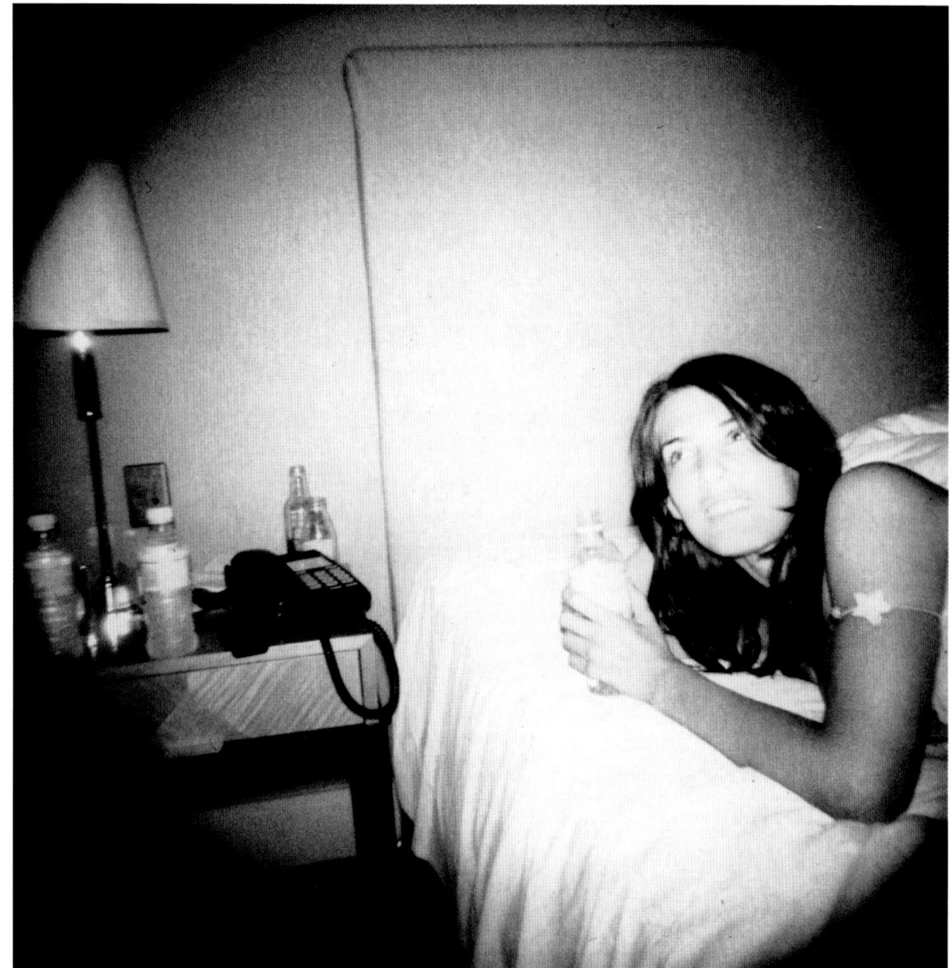

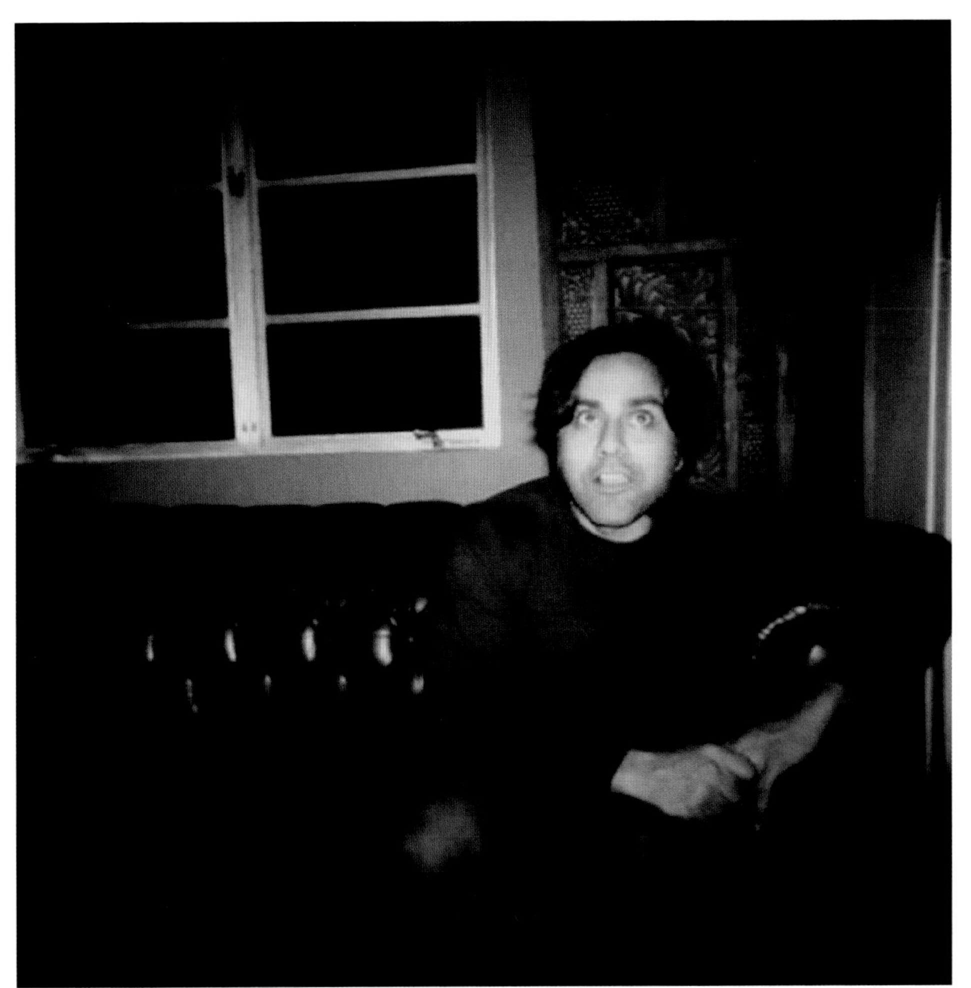

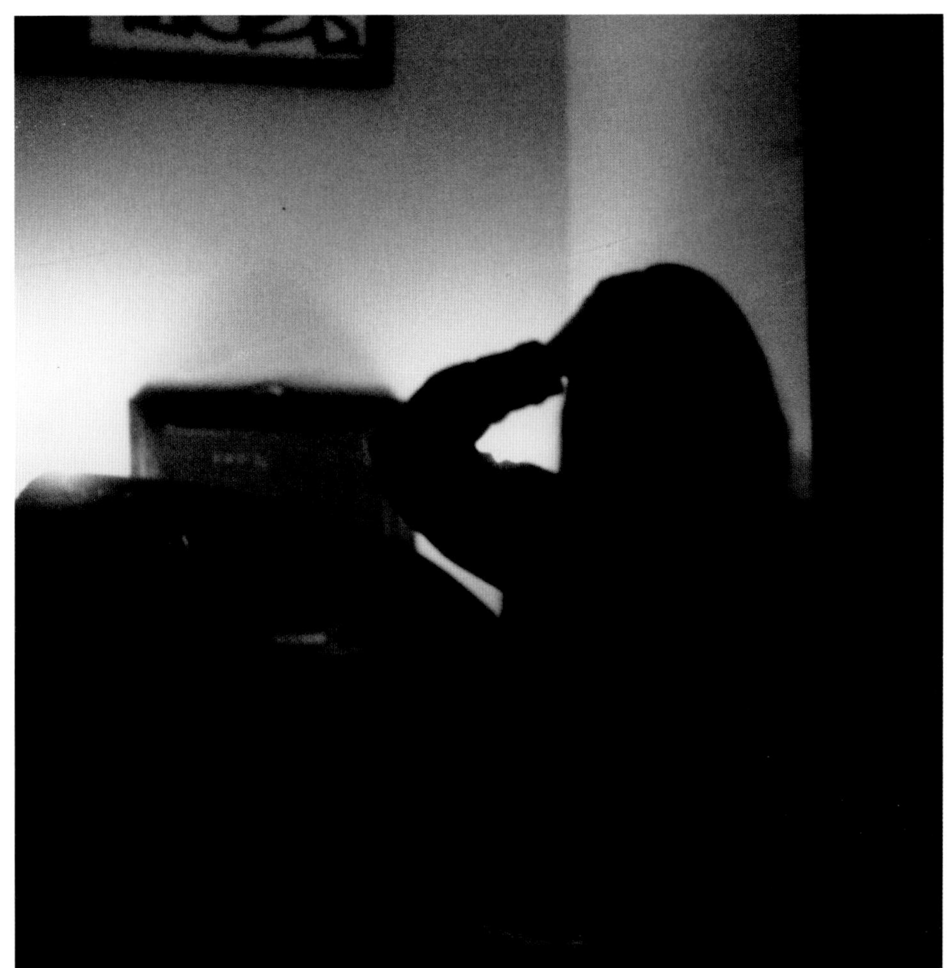

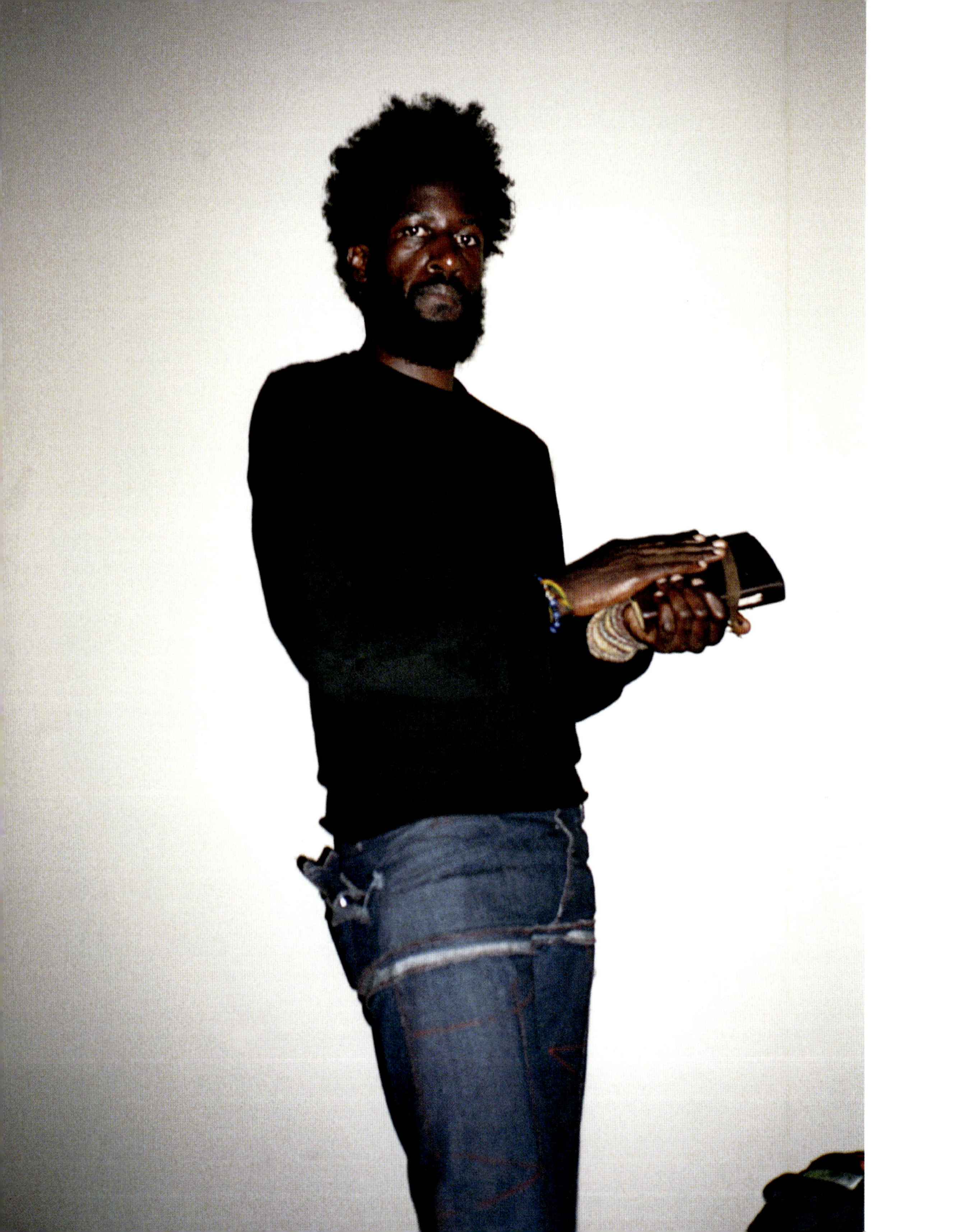

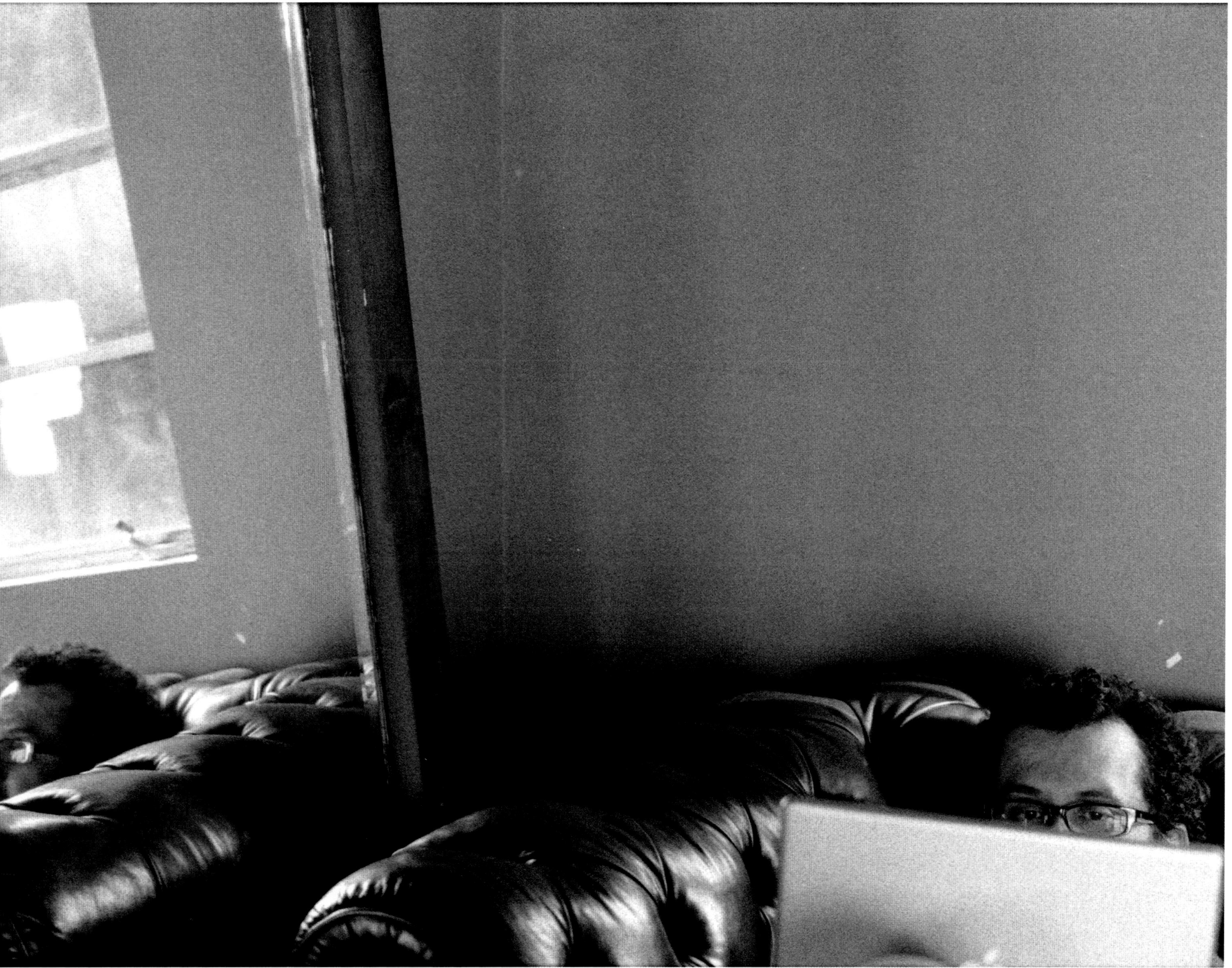

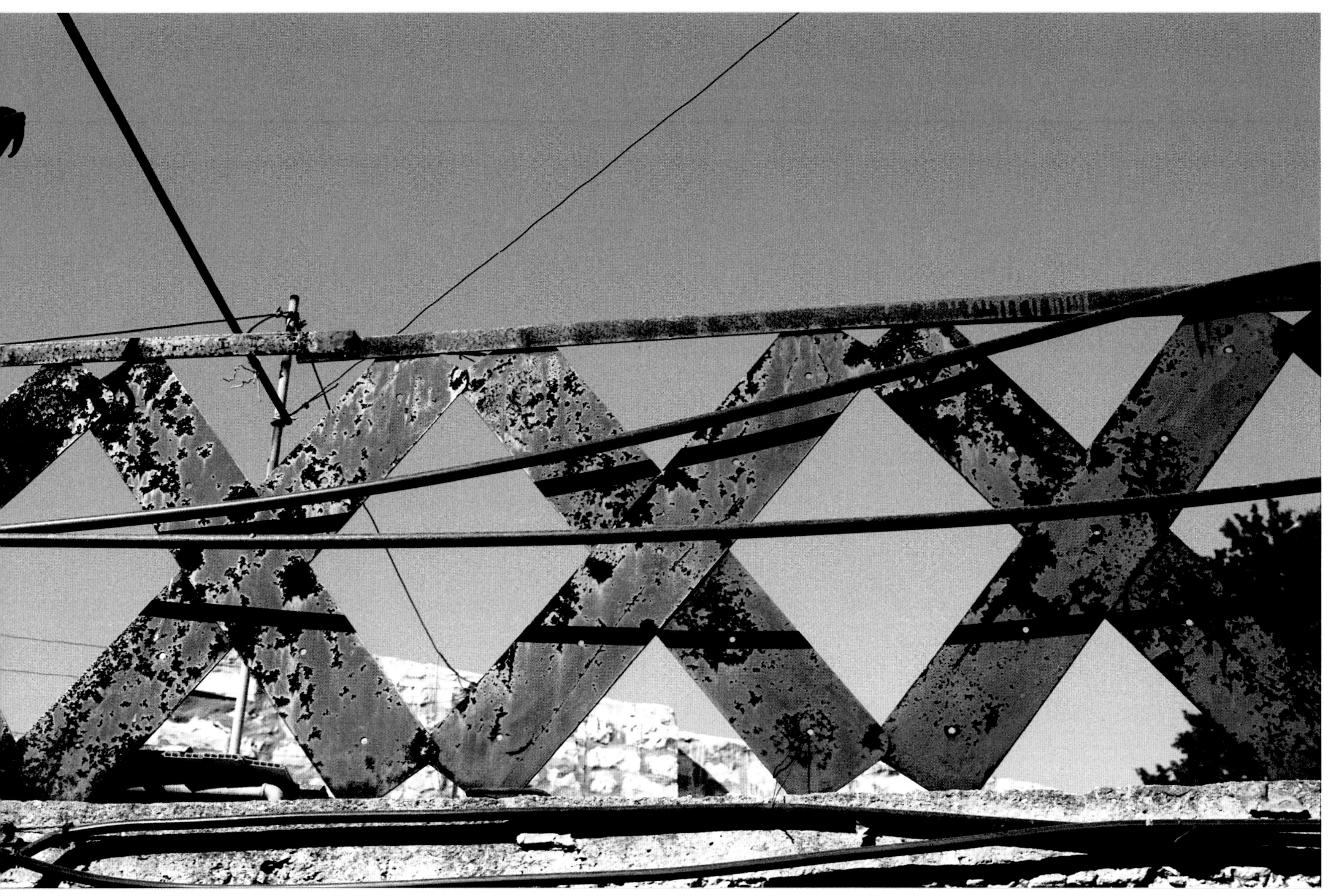

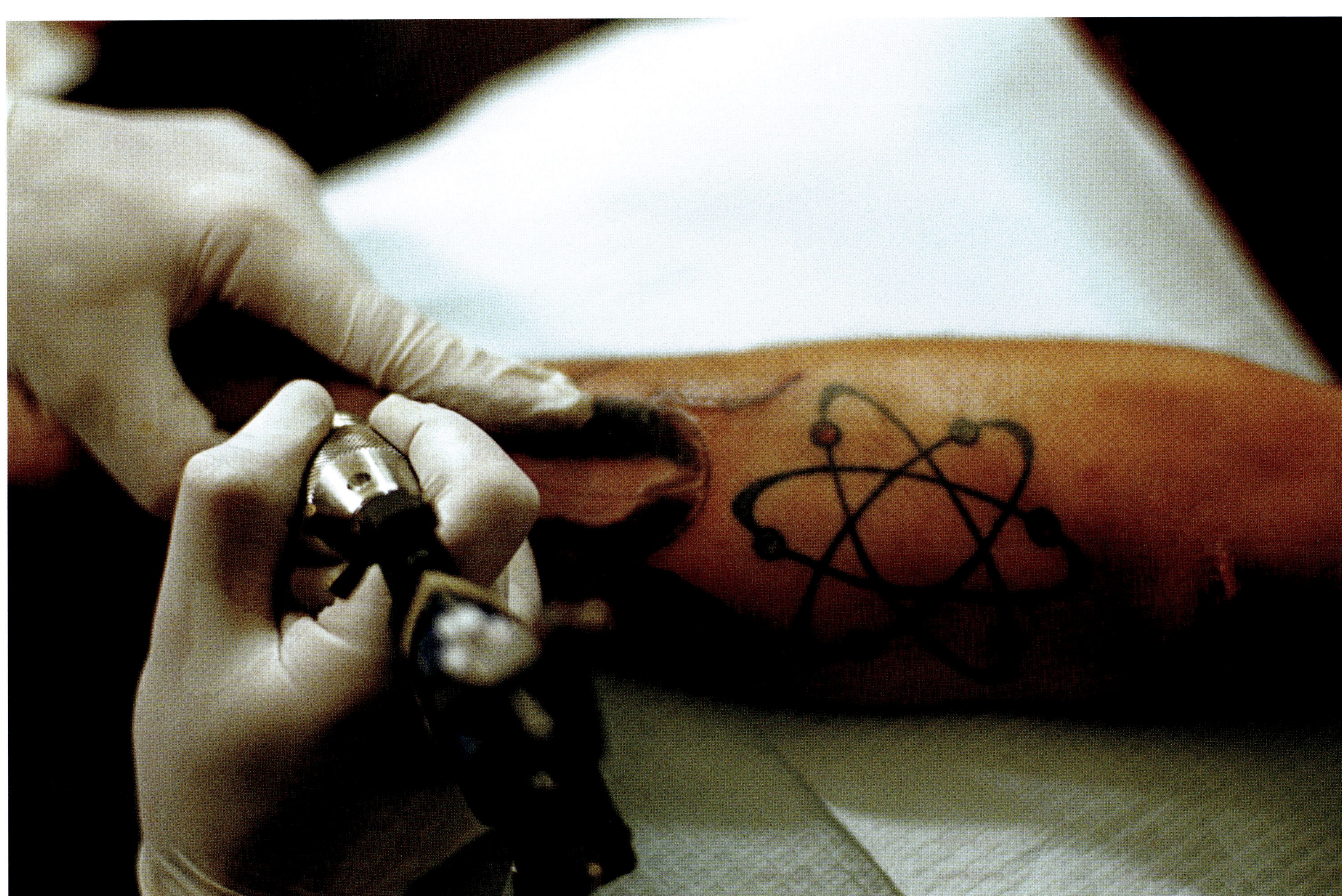

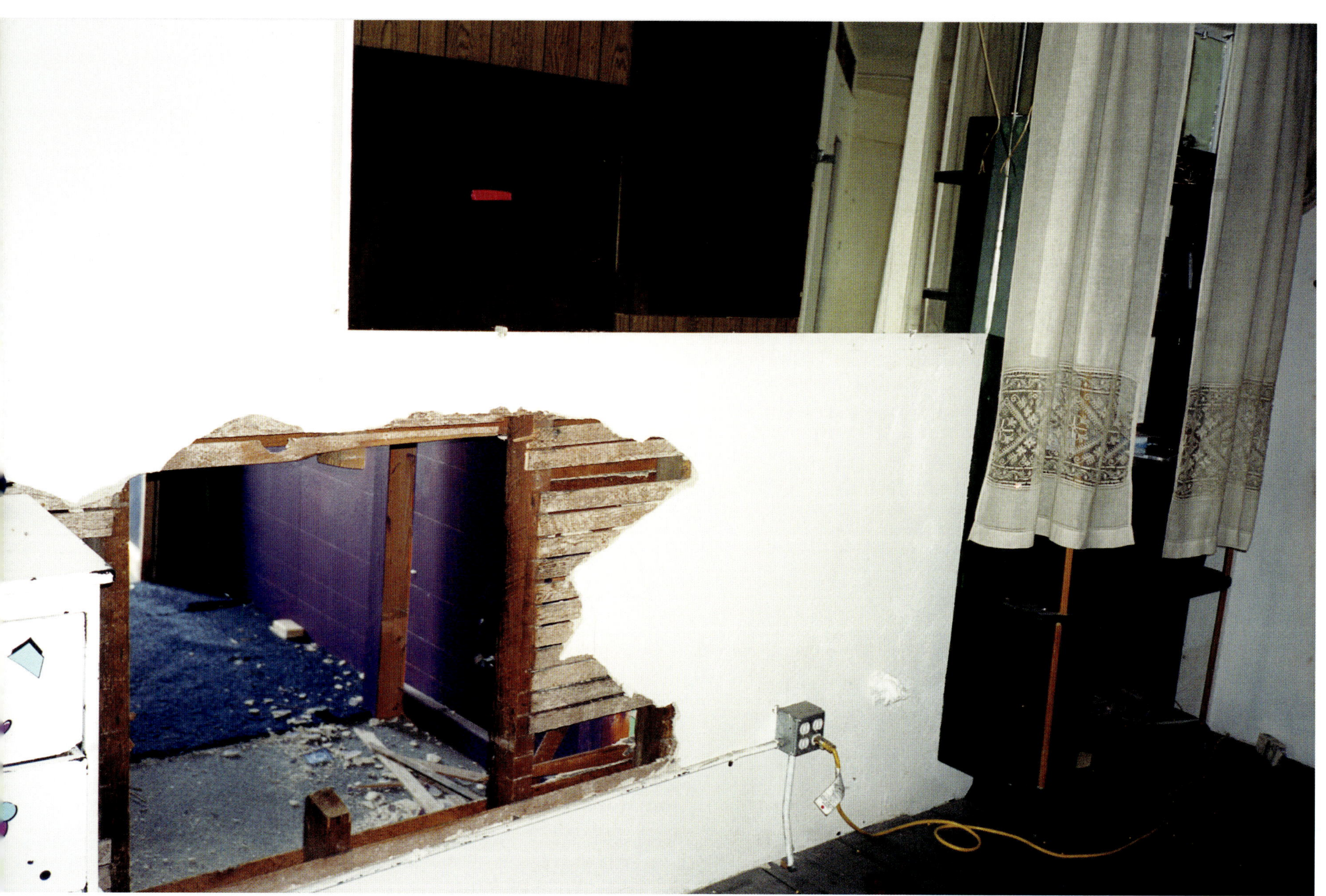

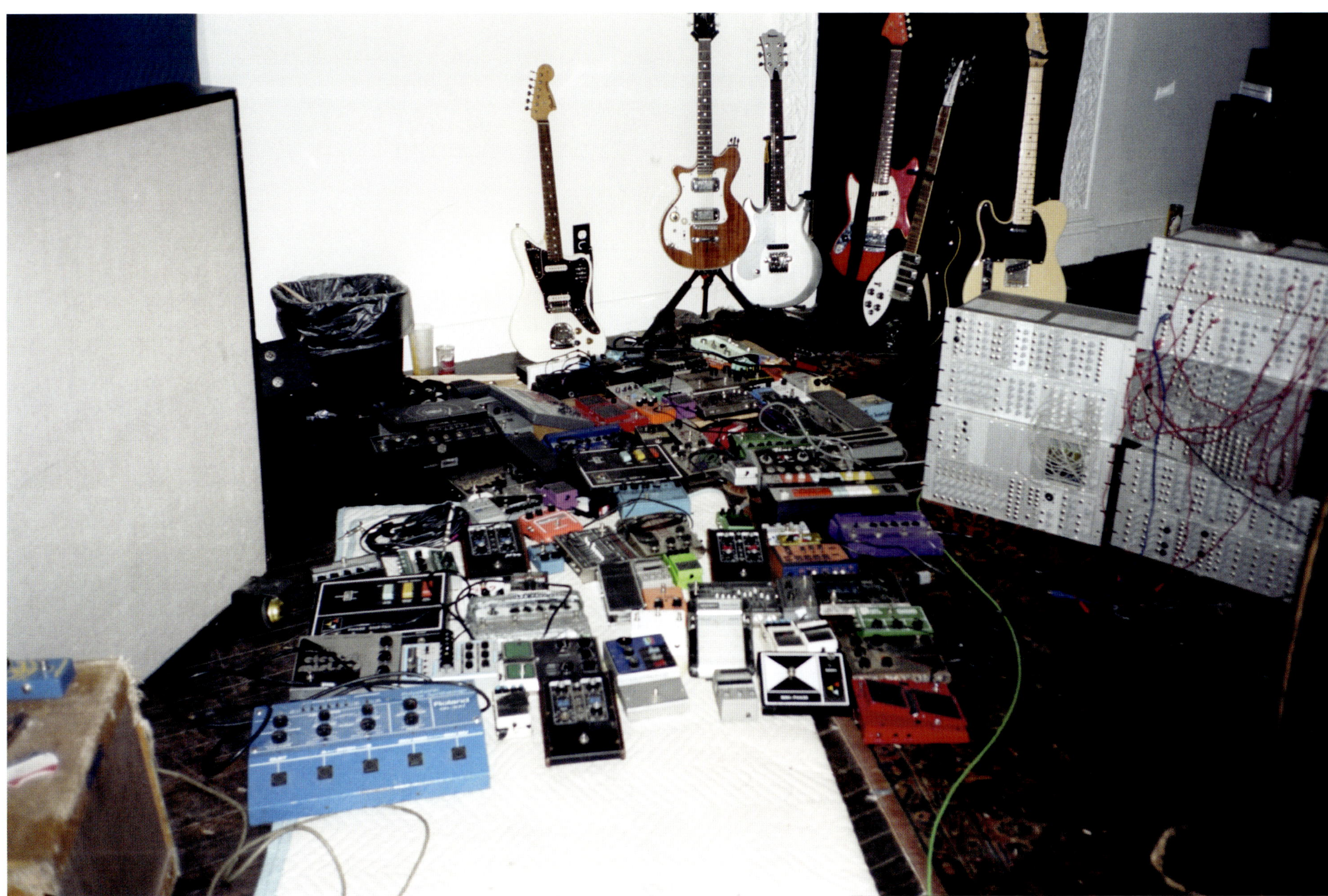

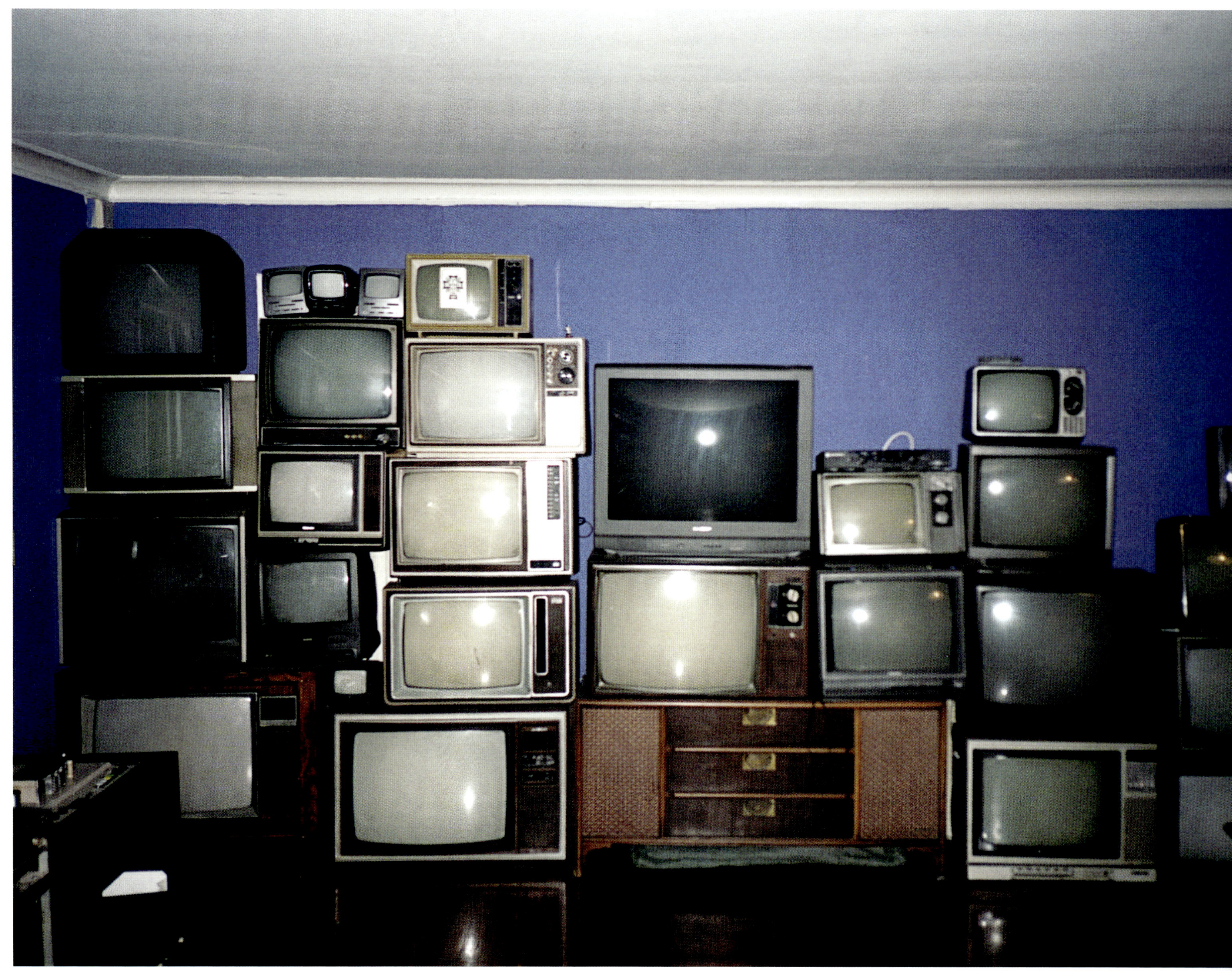

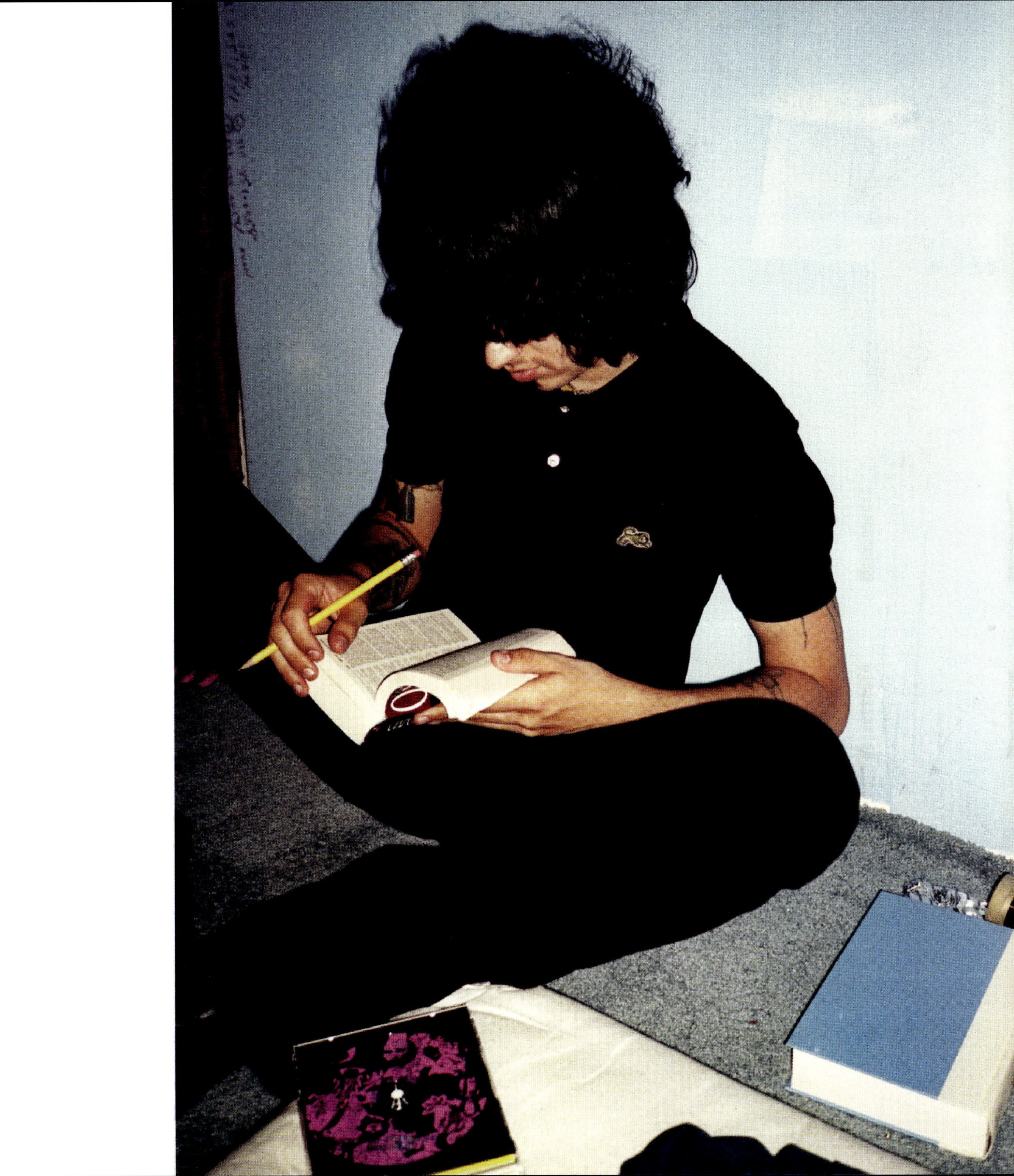

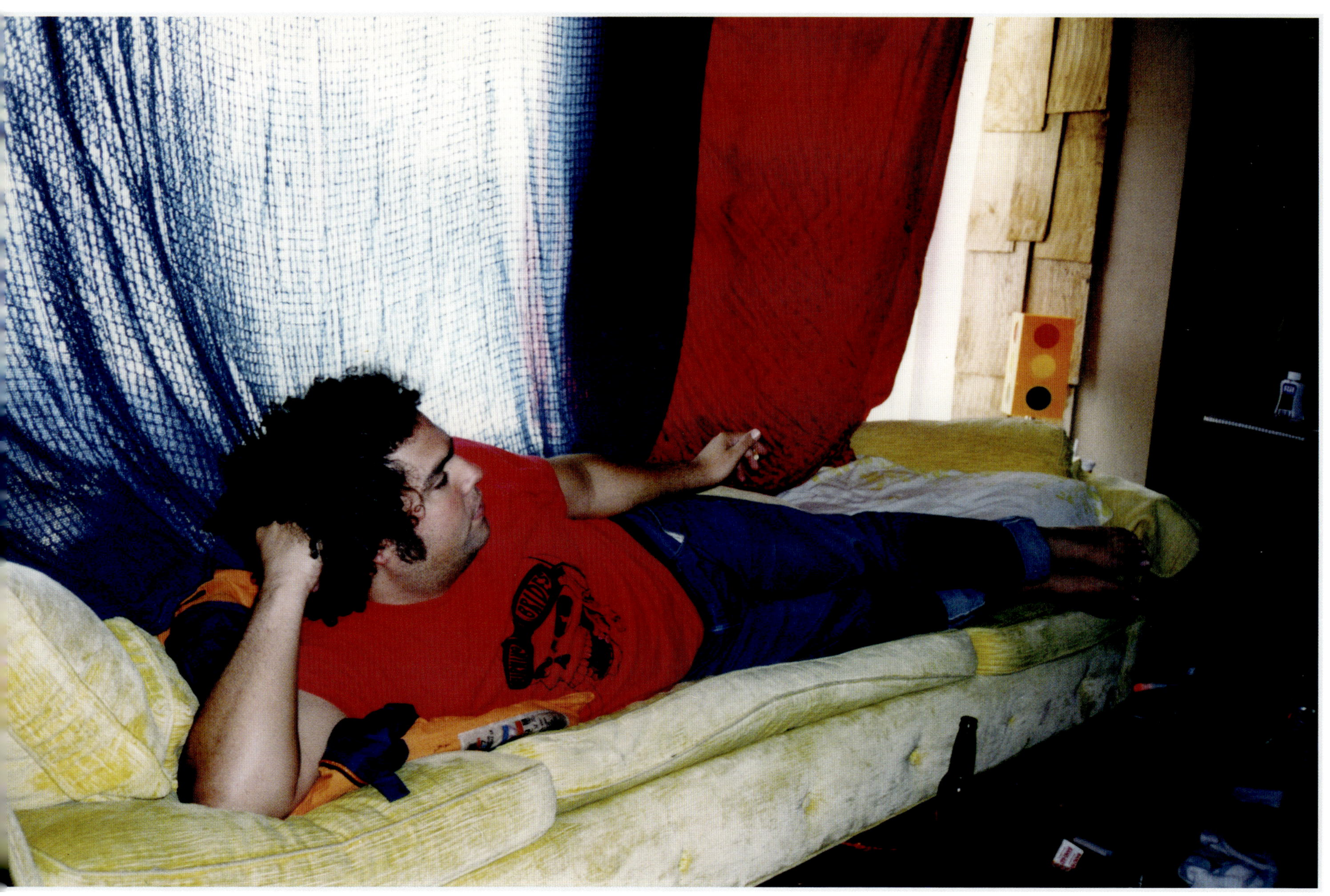

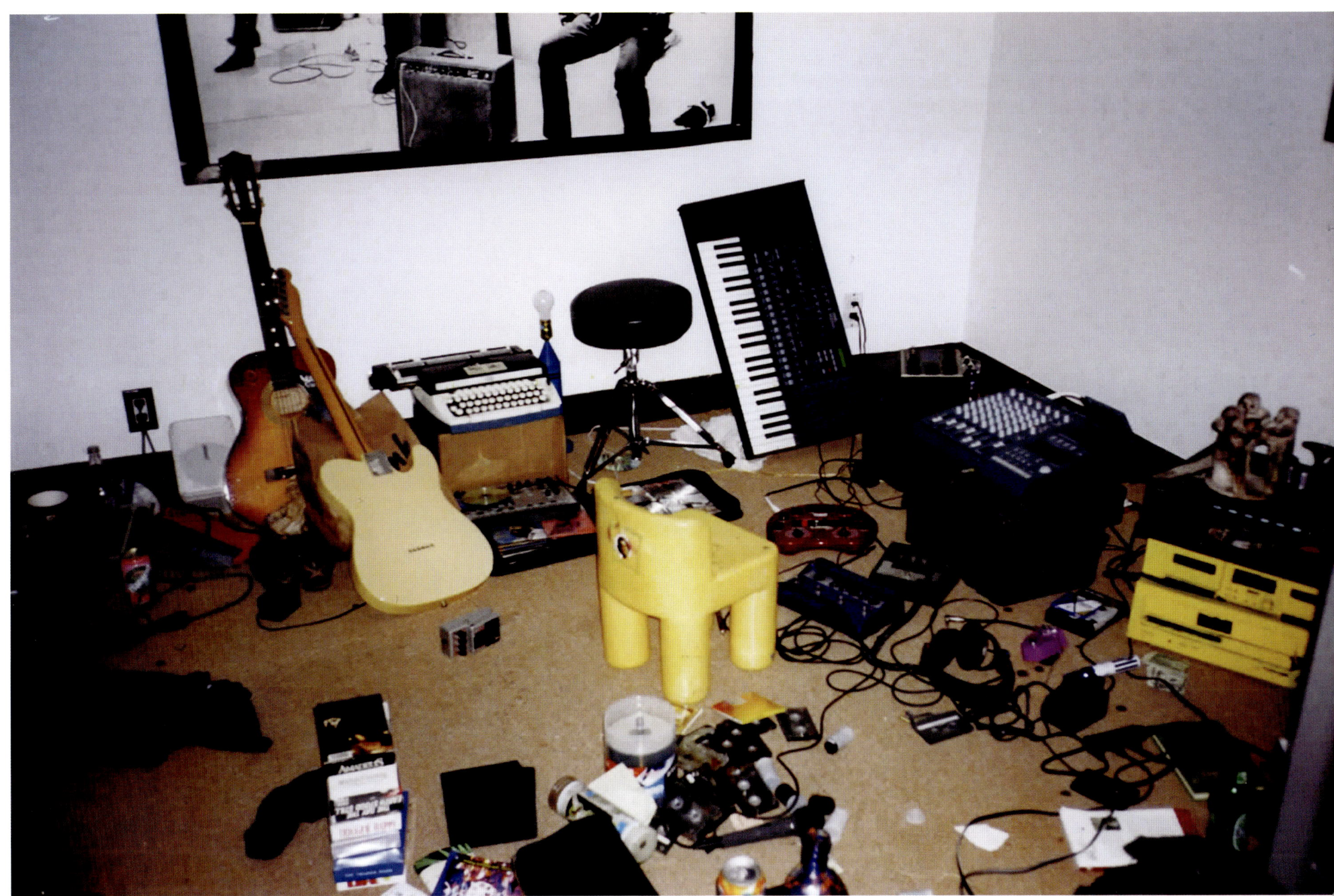

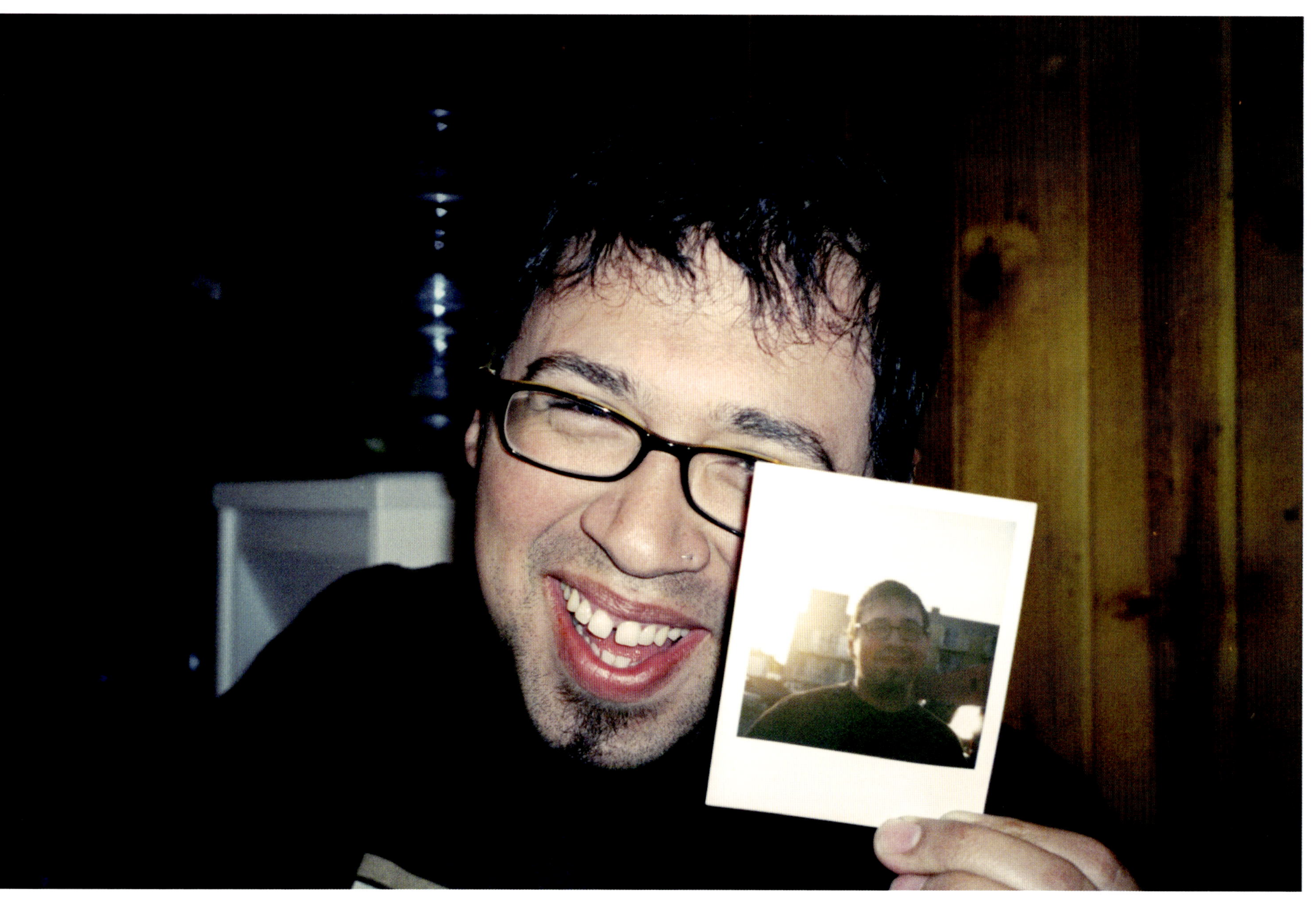

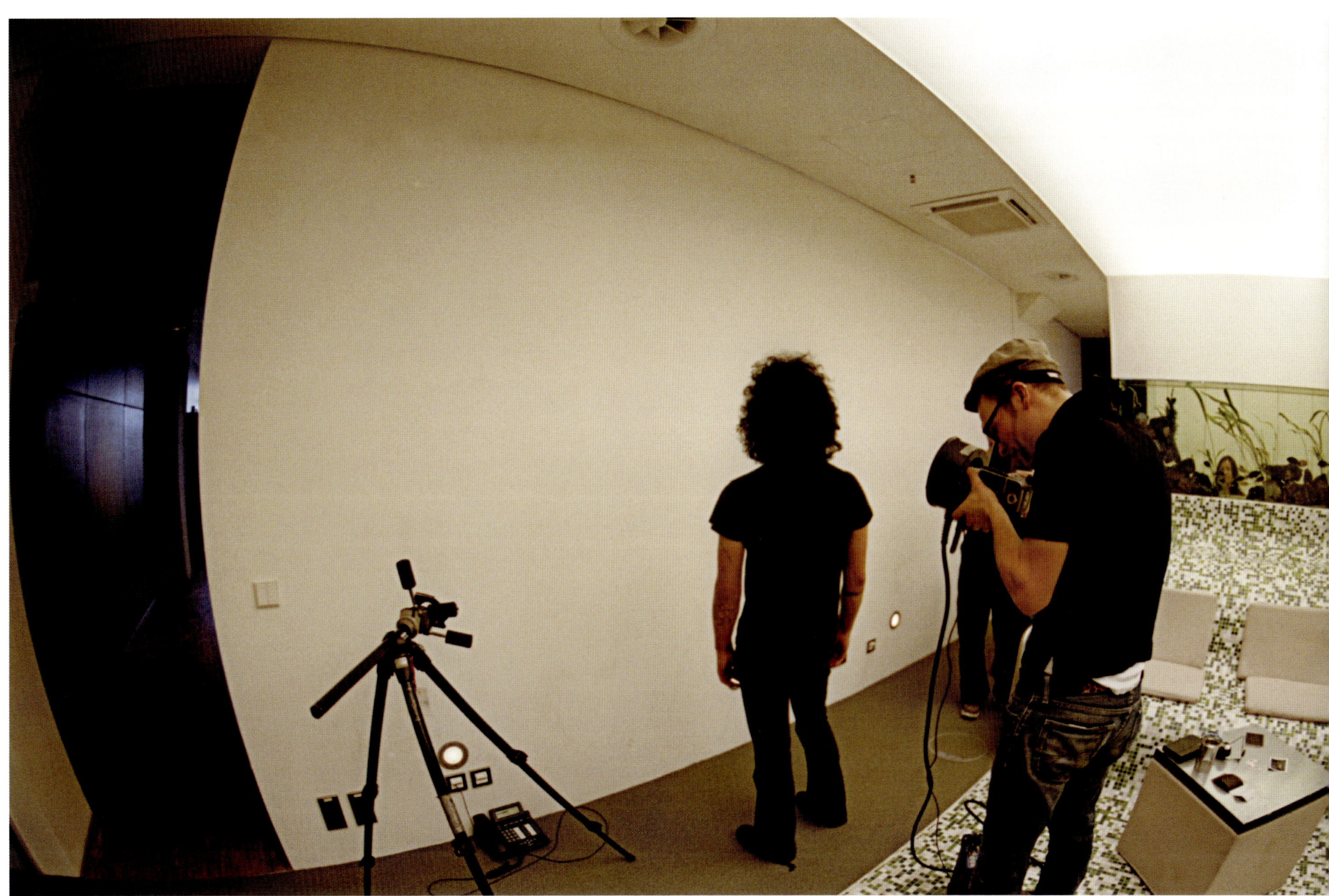

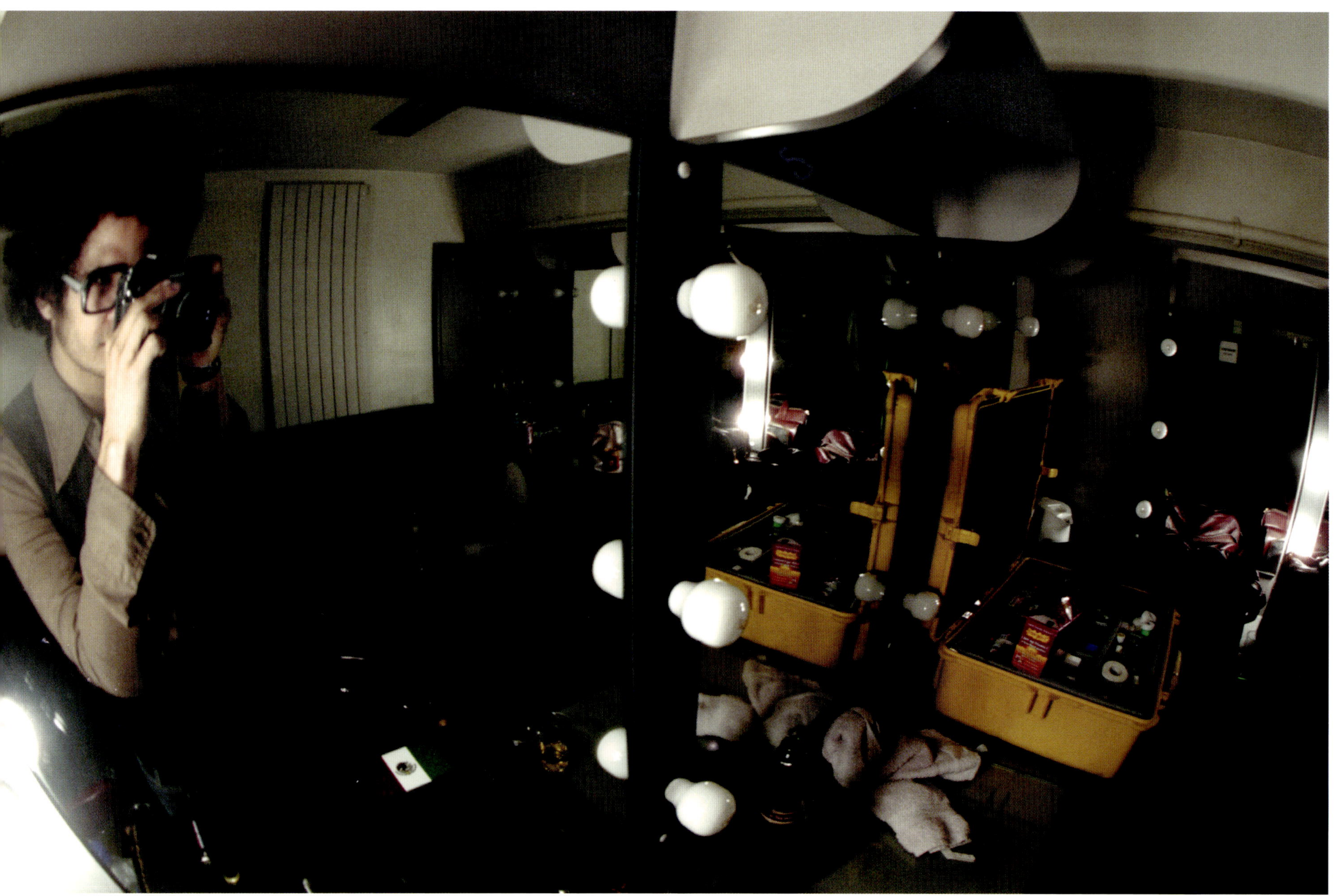

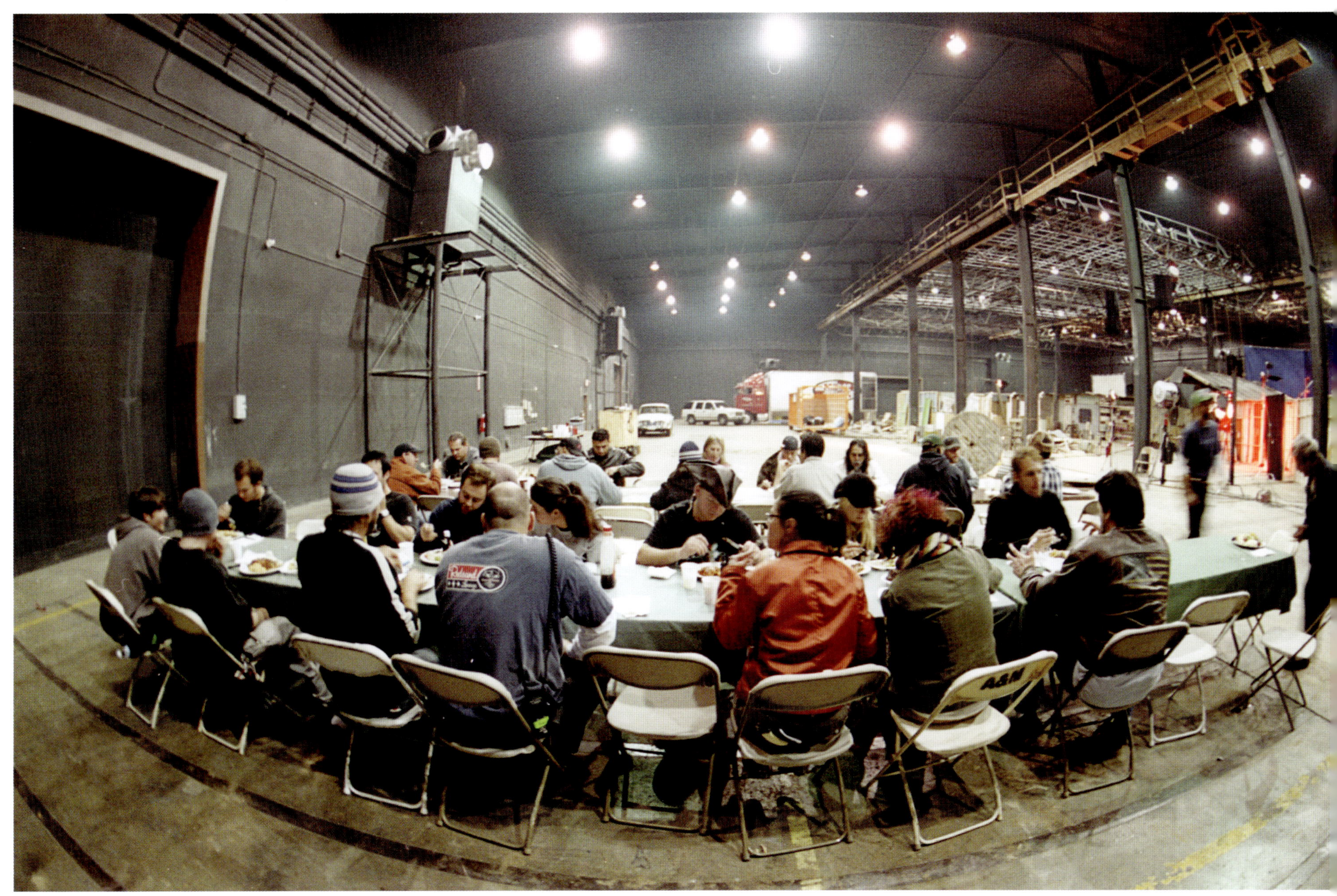
A&M

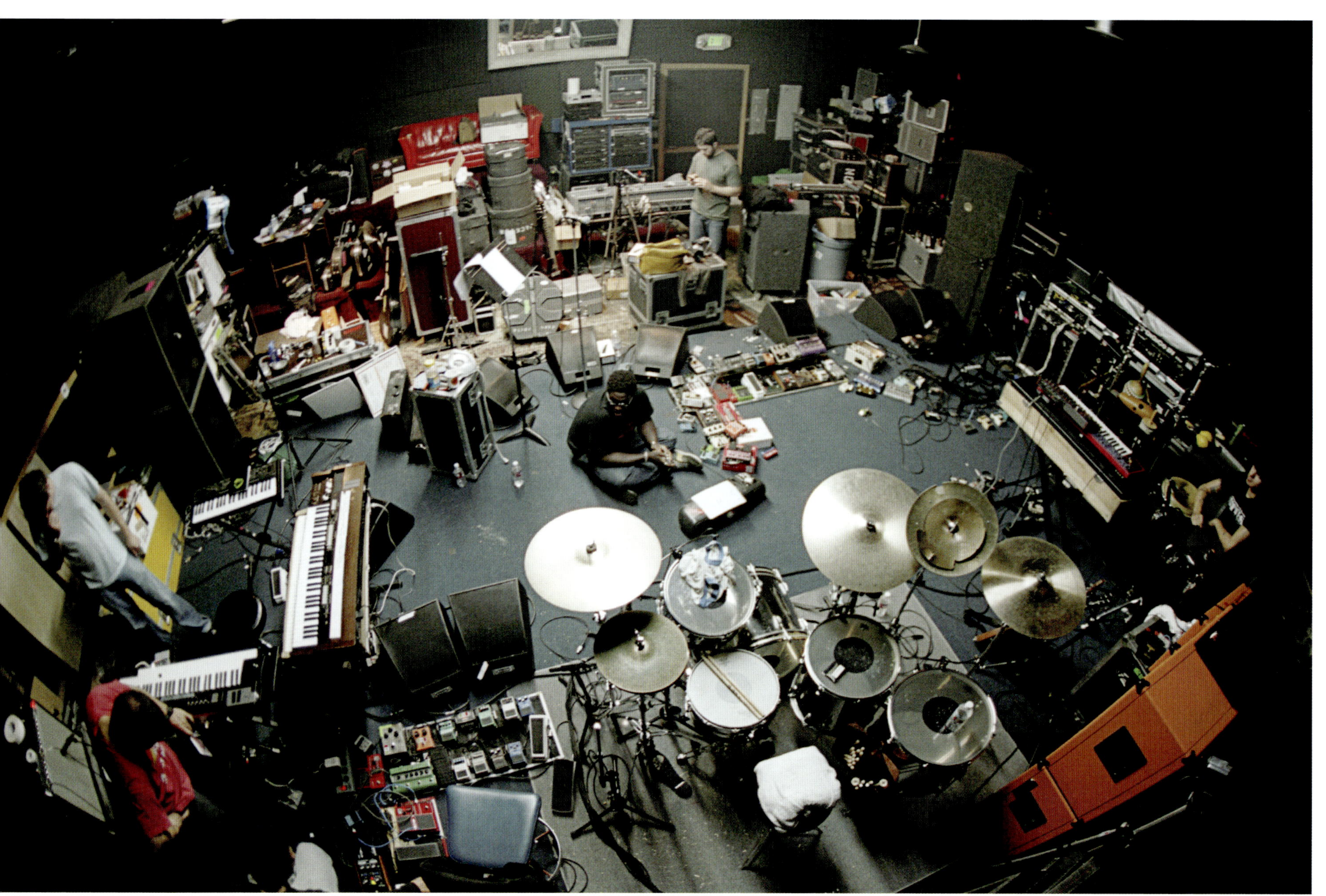

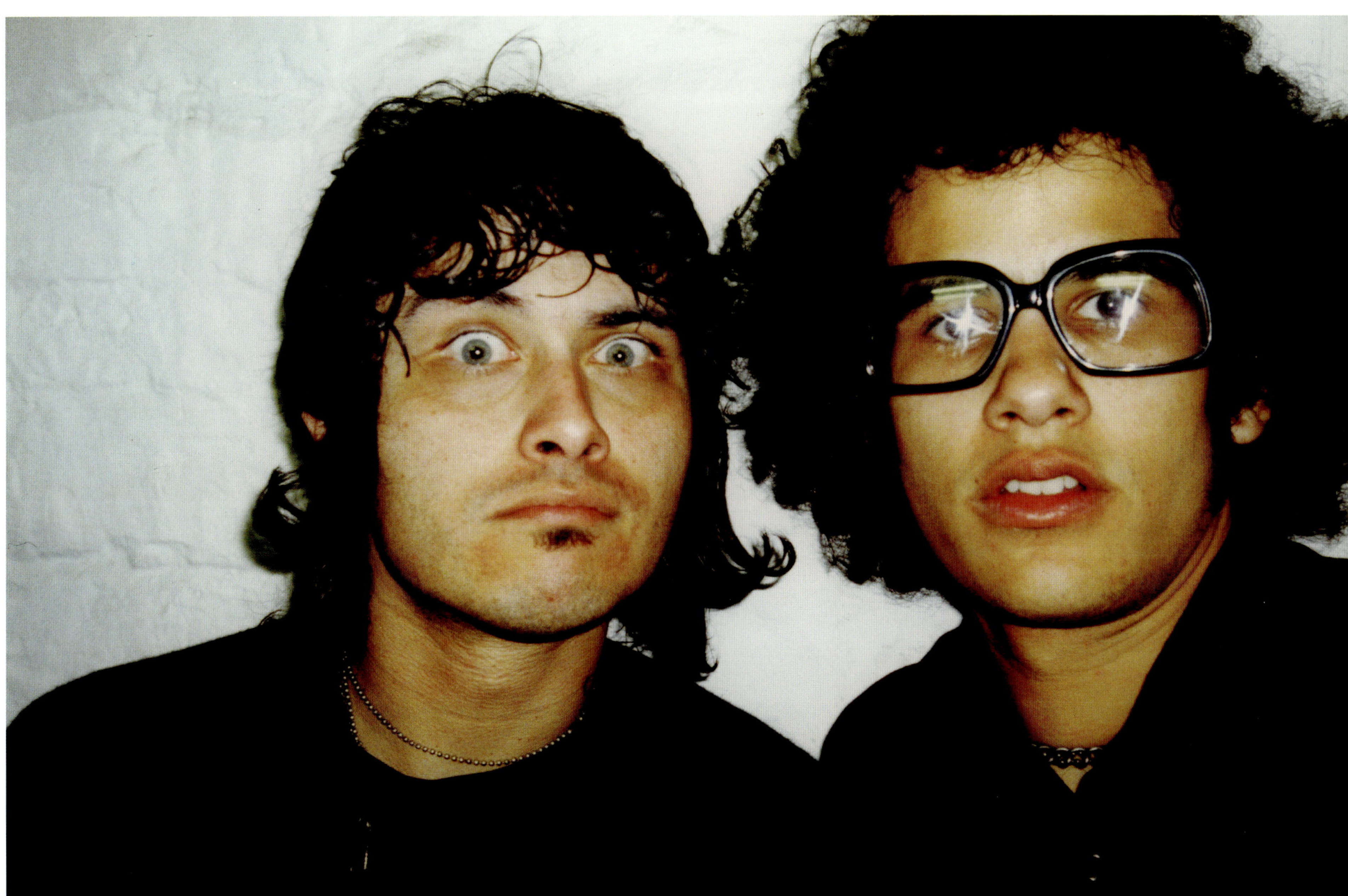

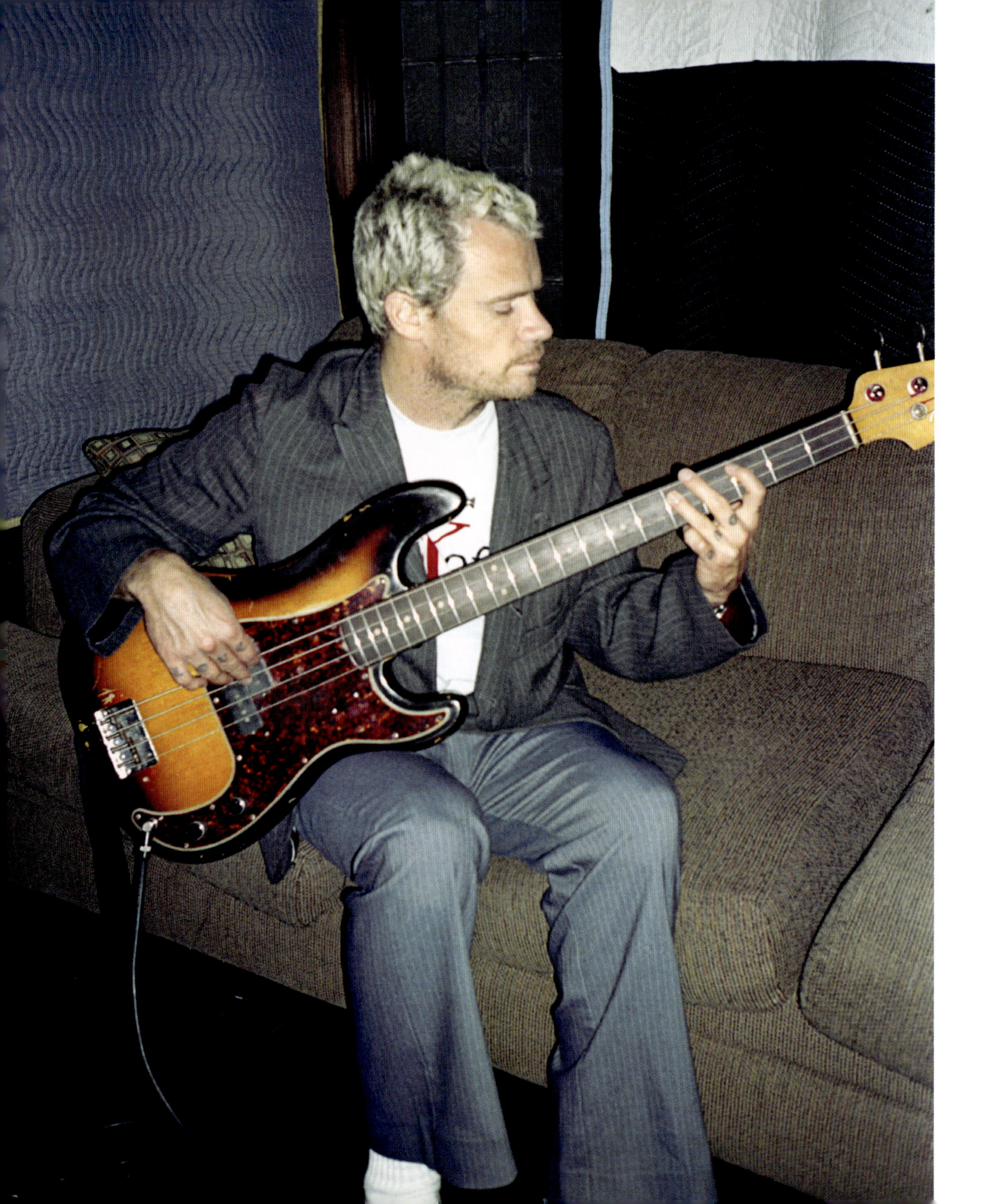

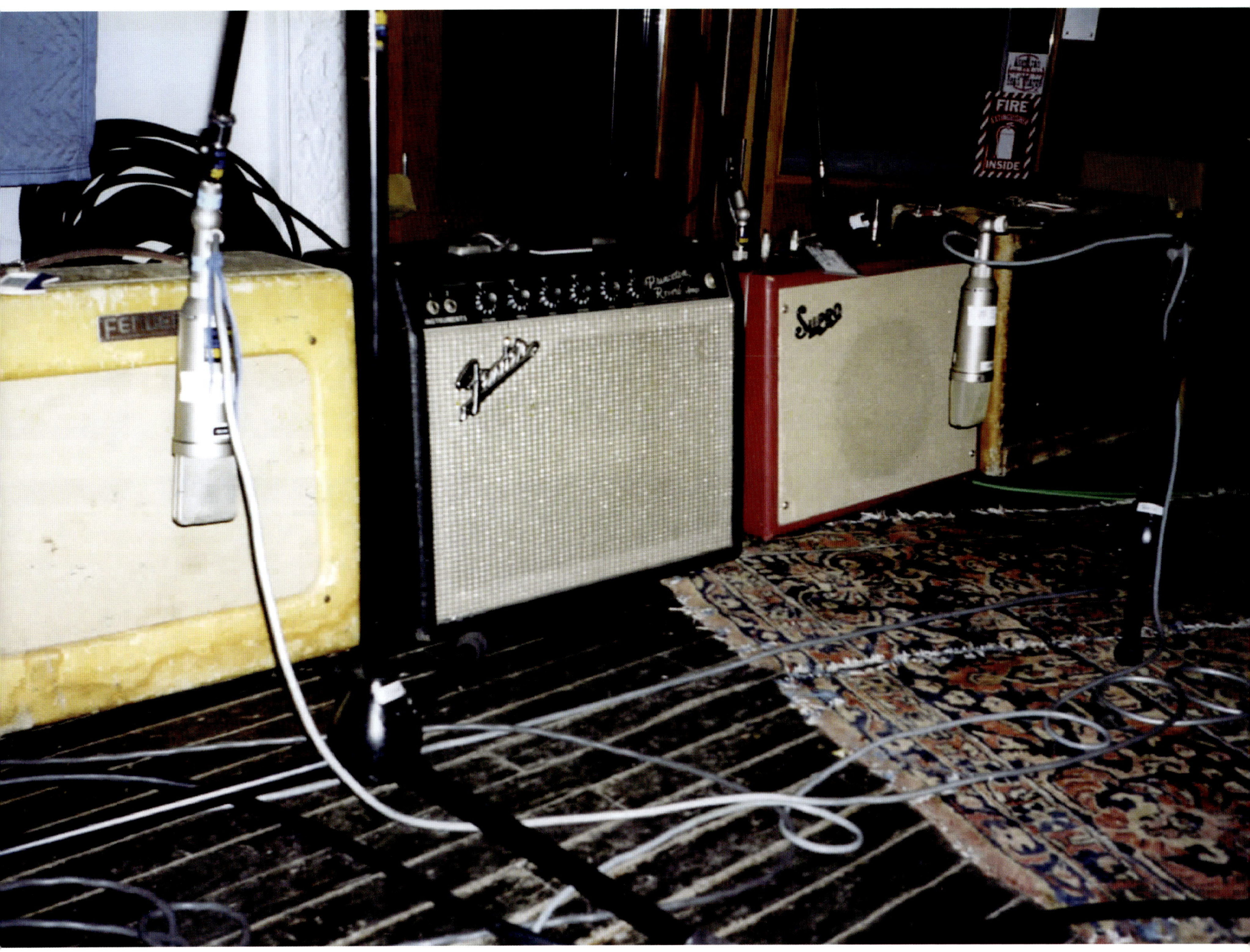
Fender
Supro
FIRE
INSIDE

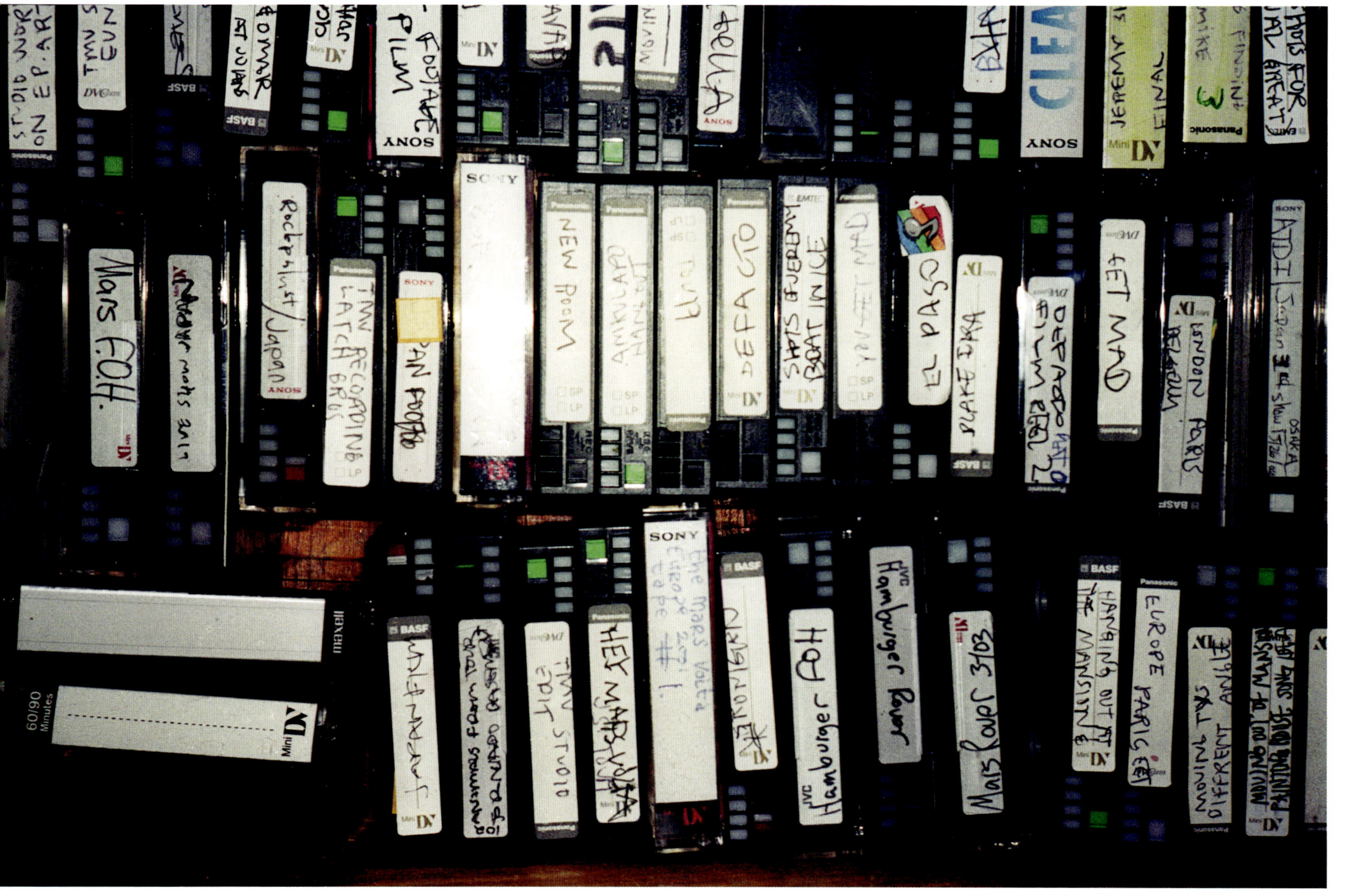

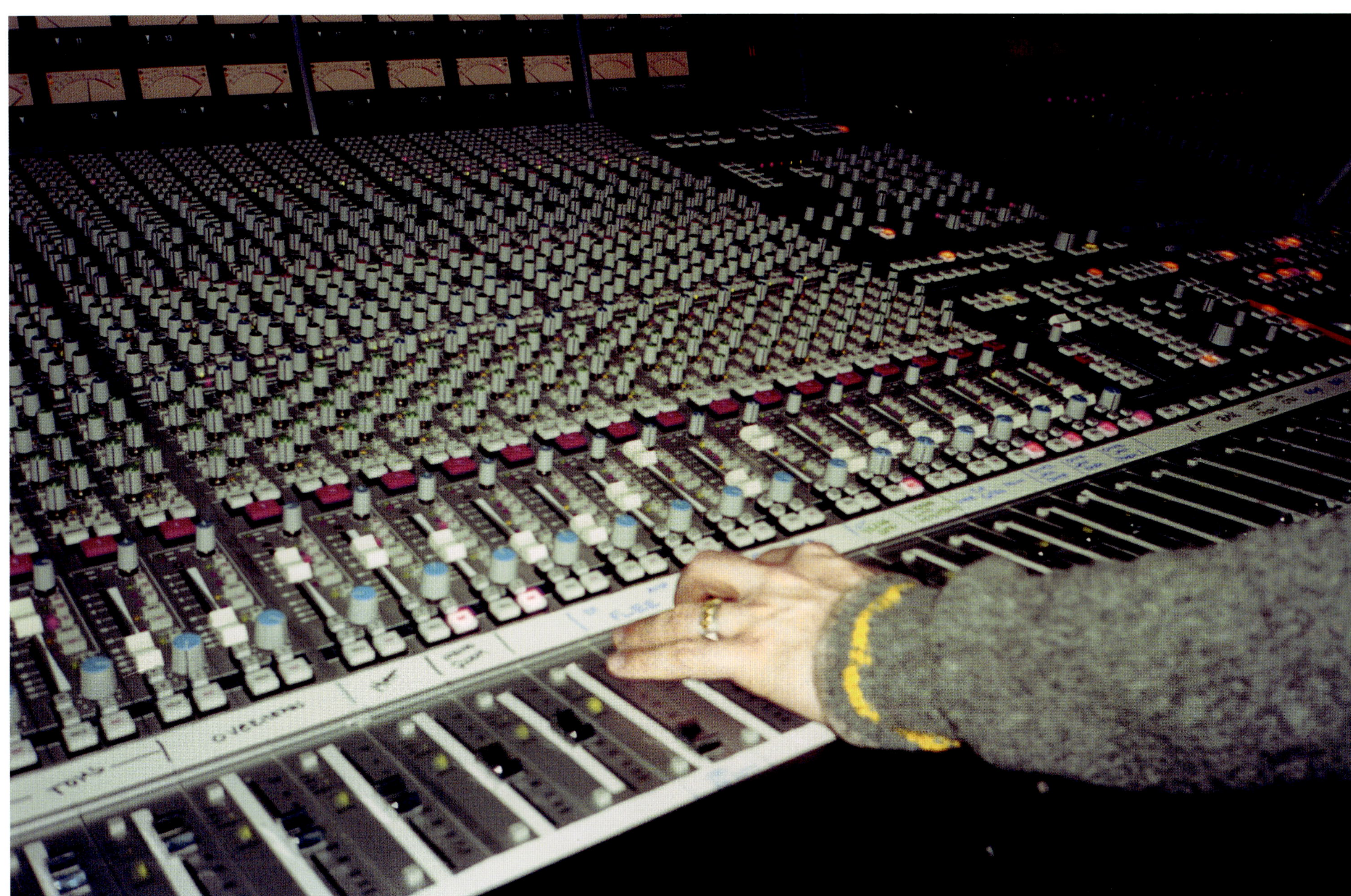

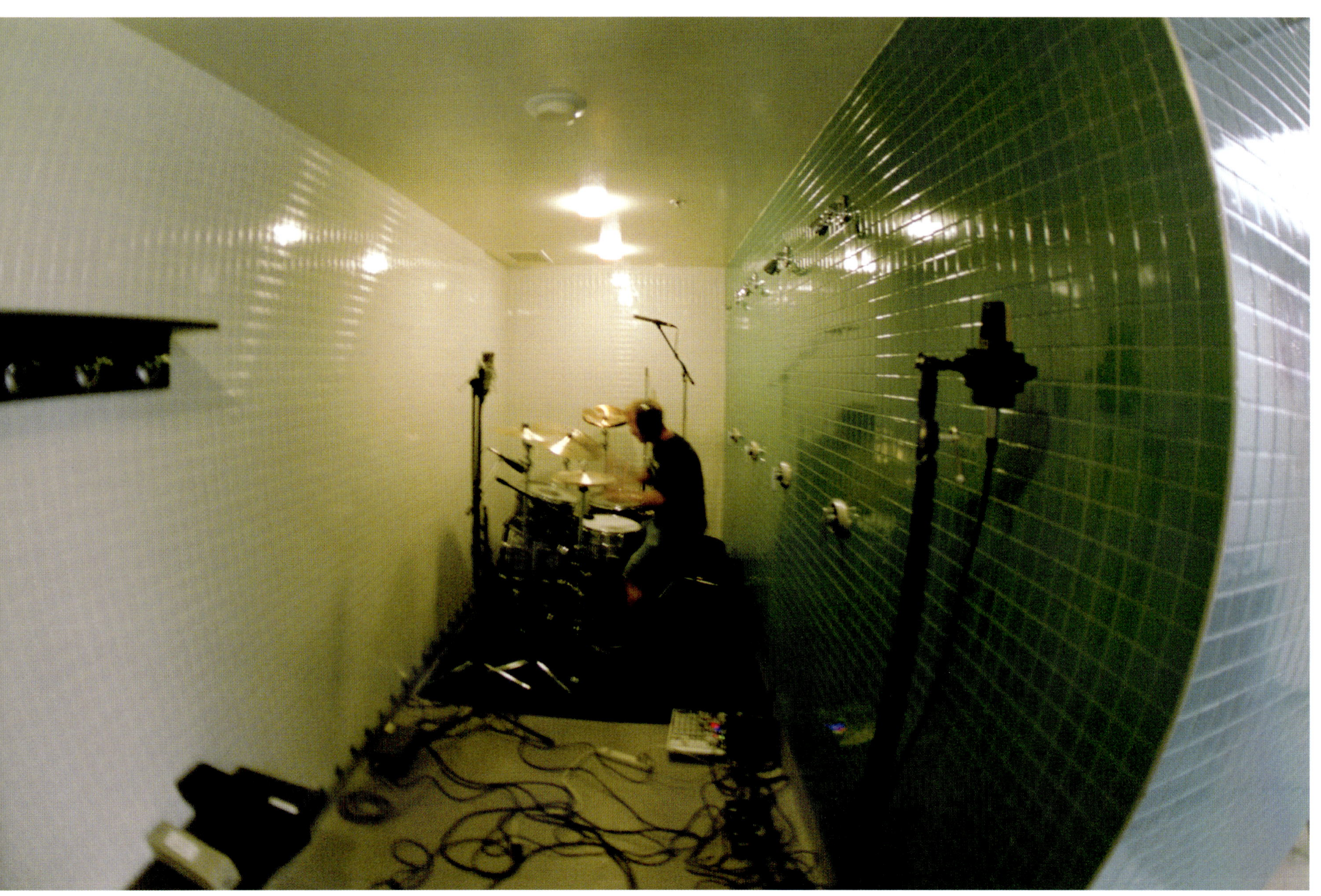

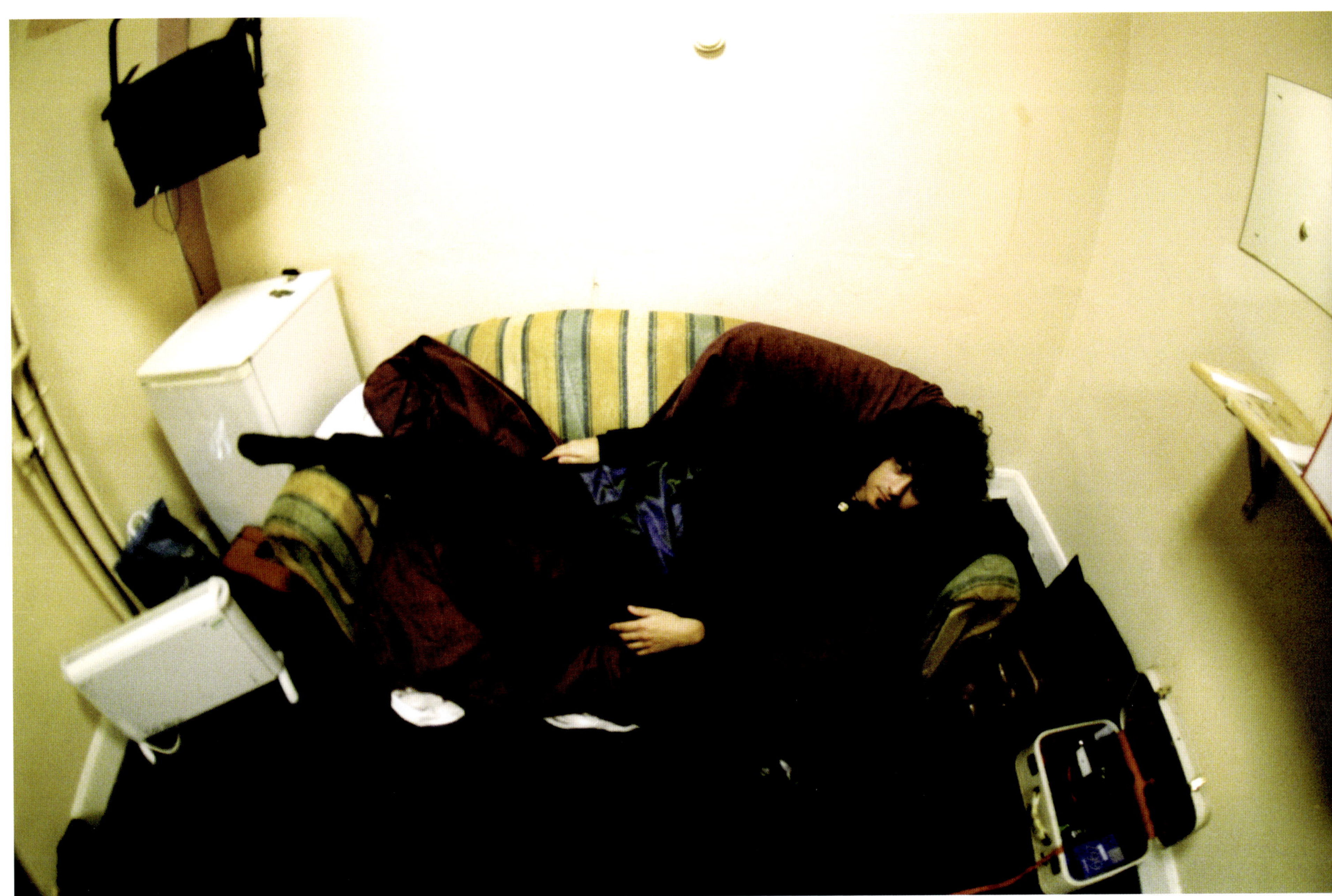

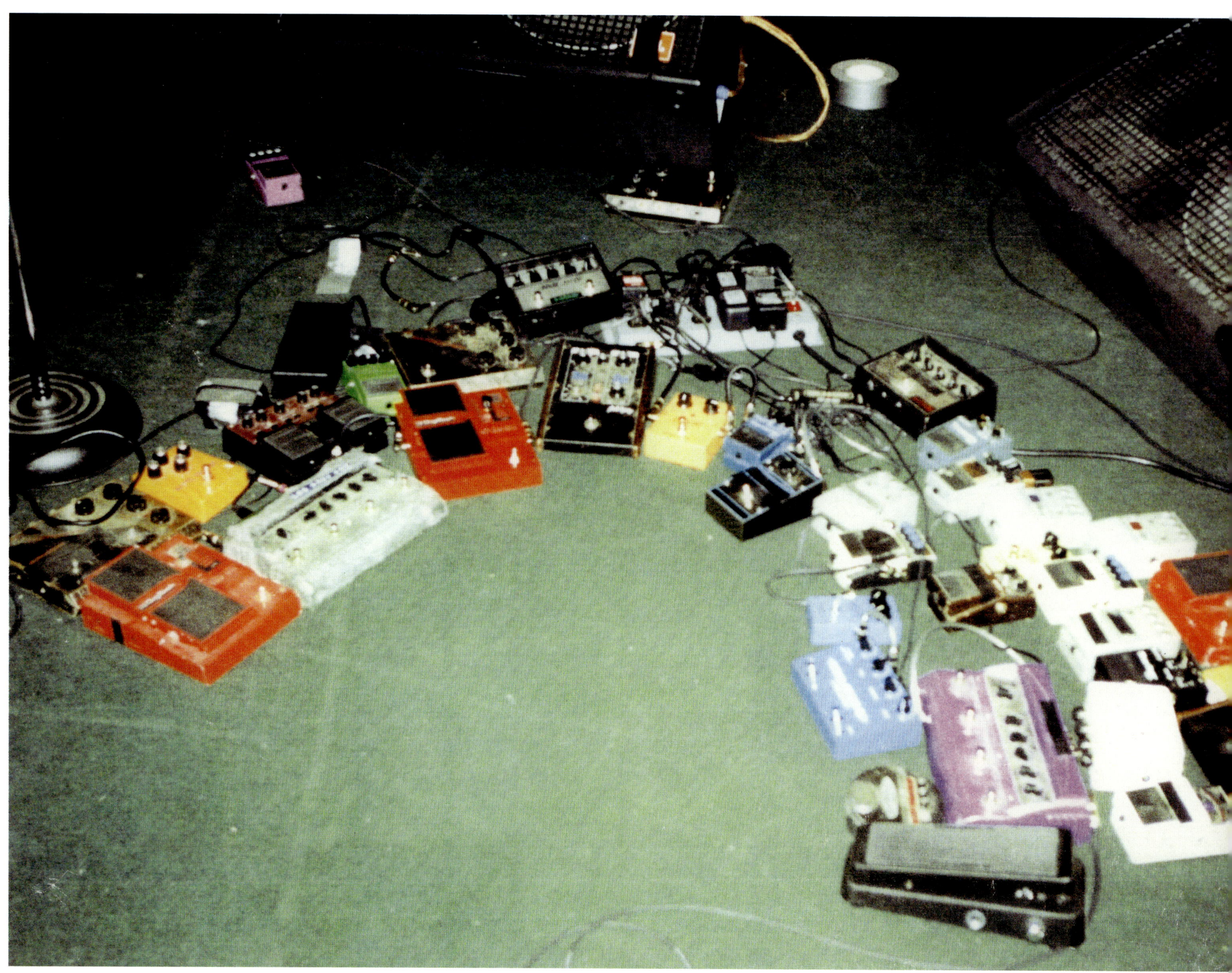

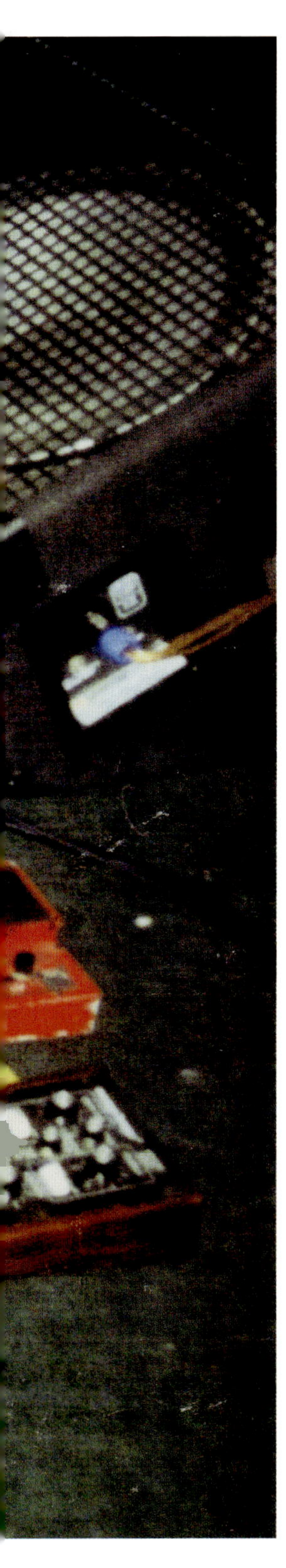

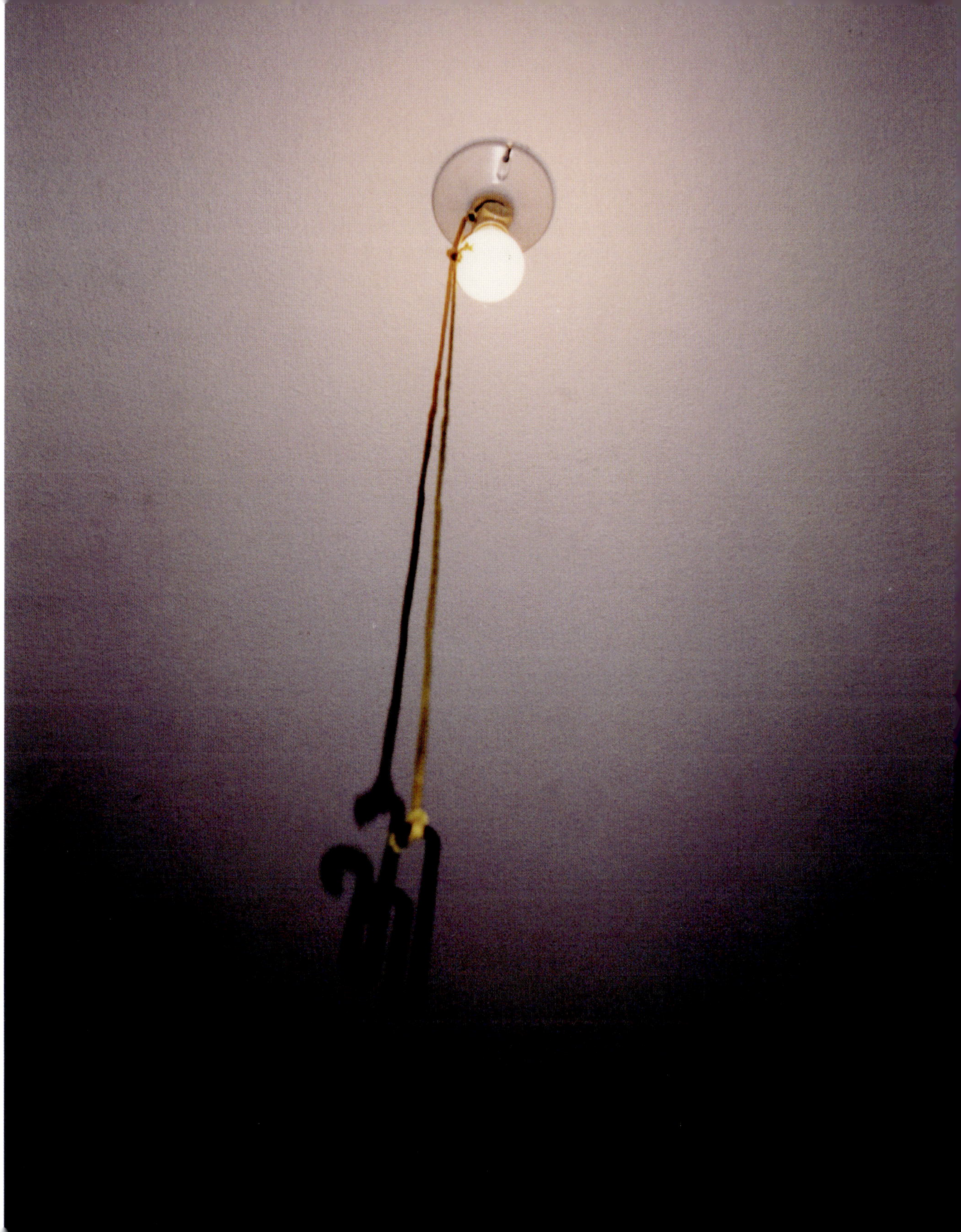

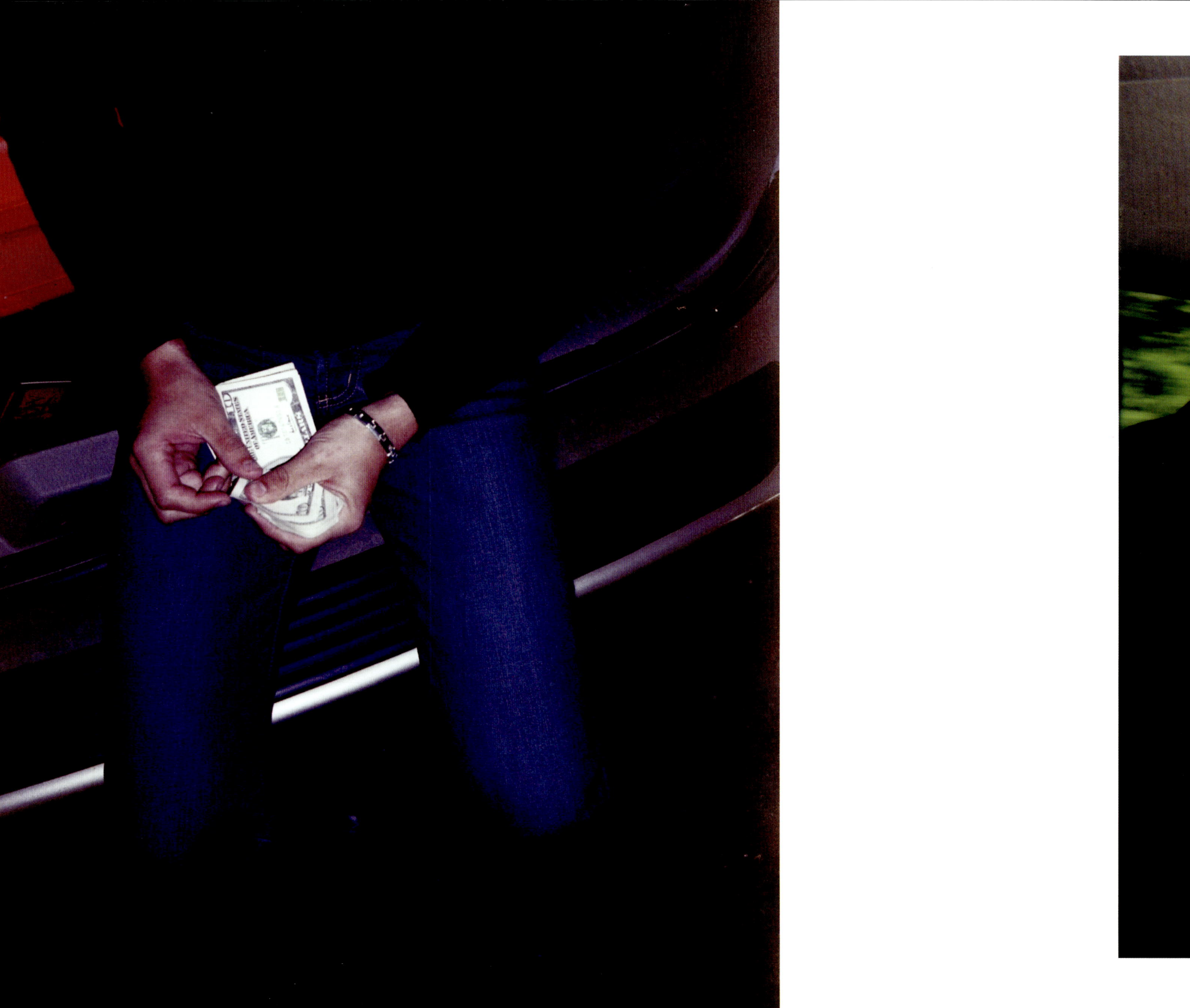

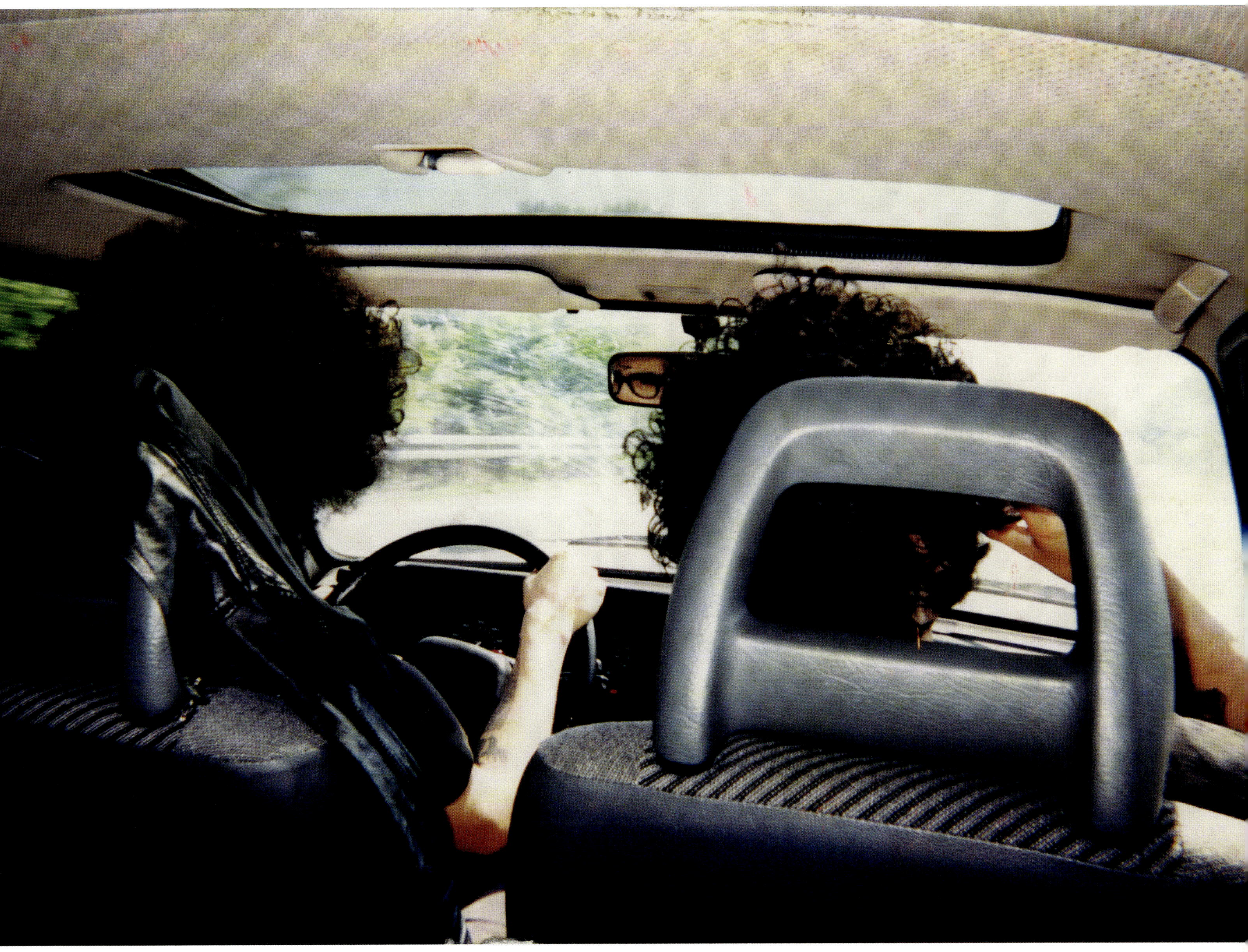

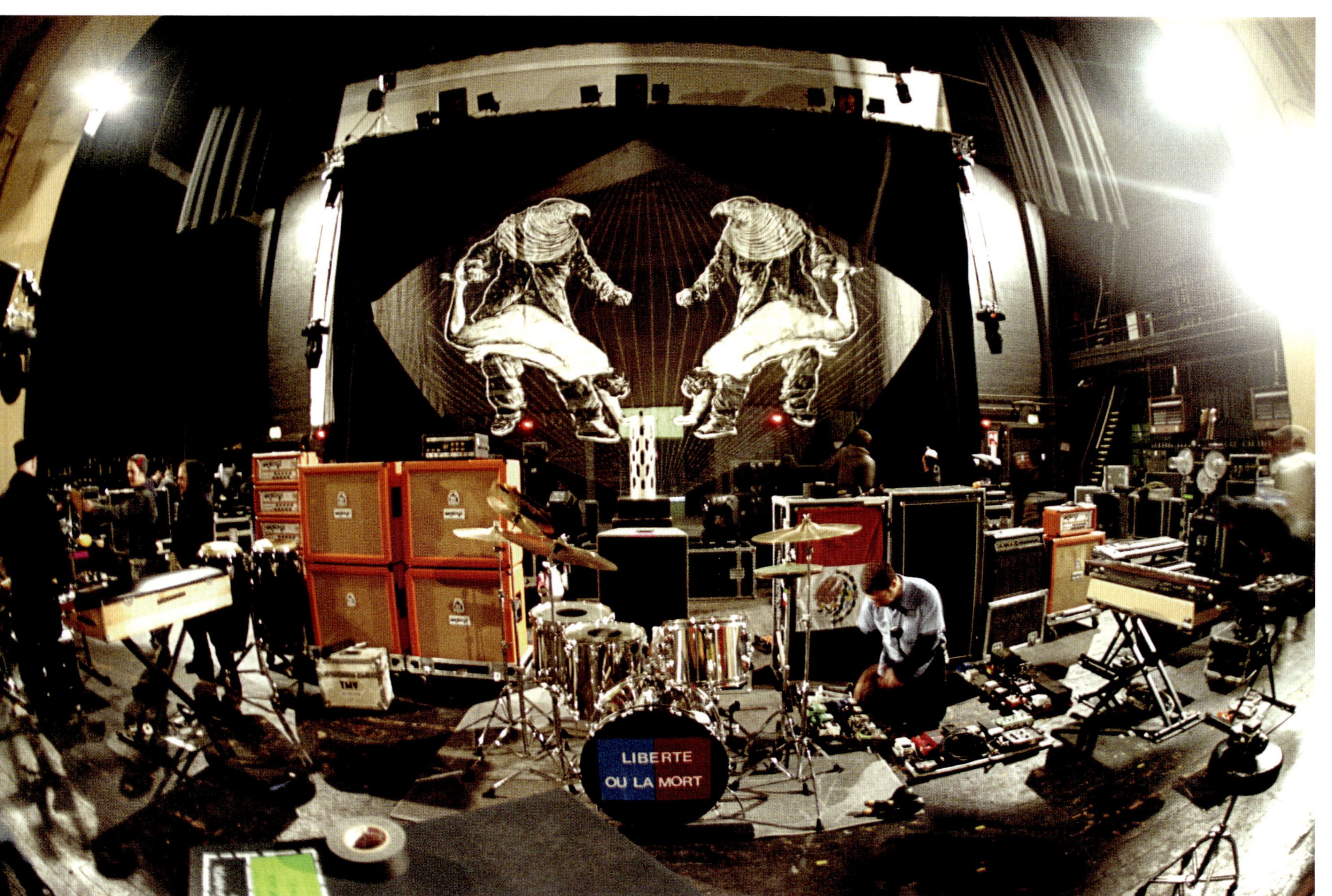
LIBERTE
OU LA MORT

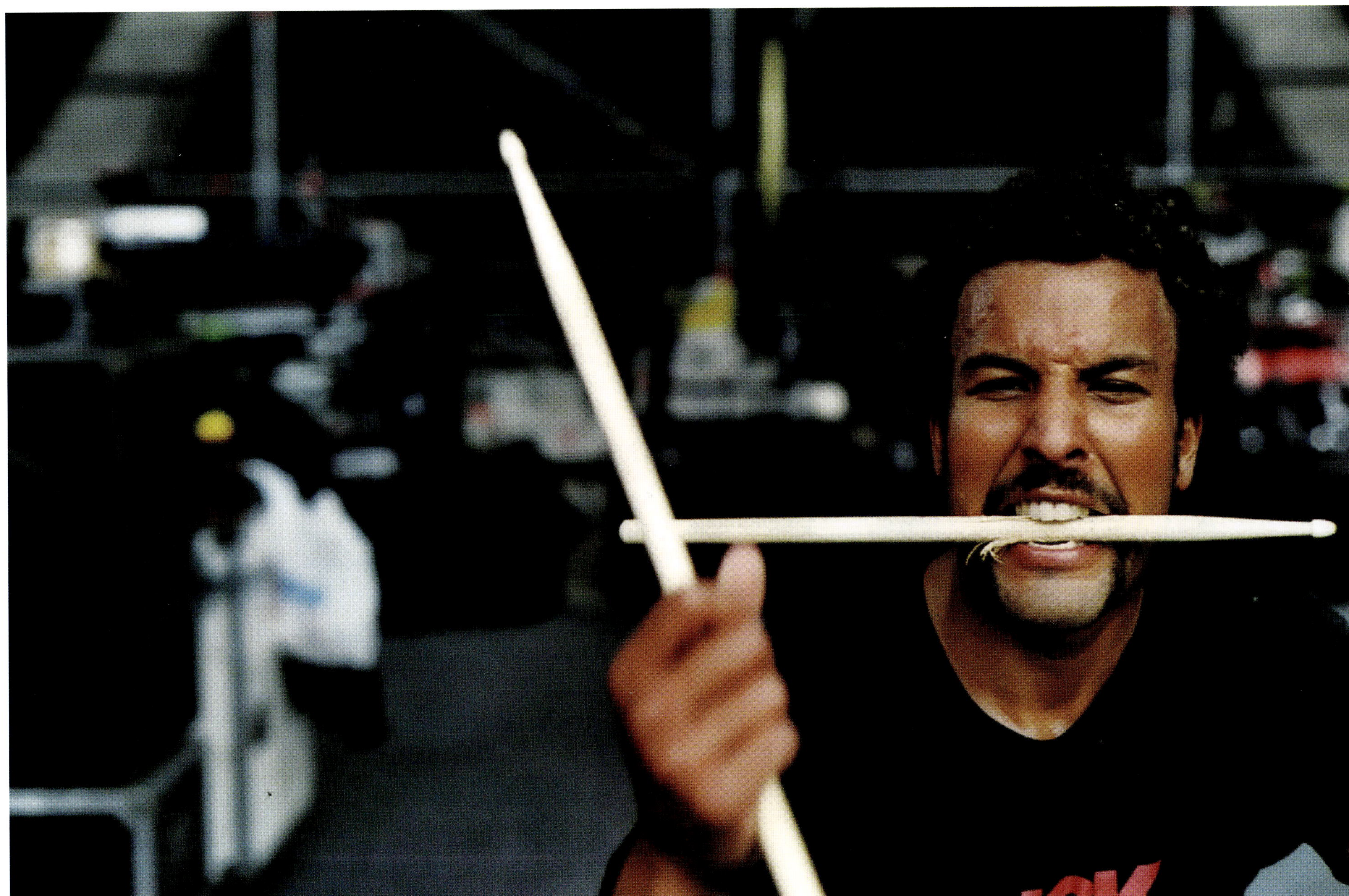

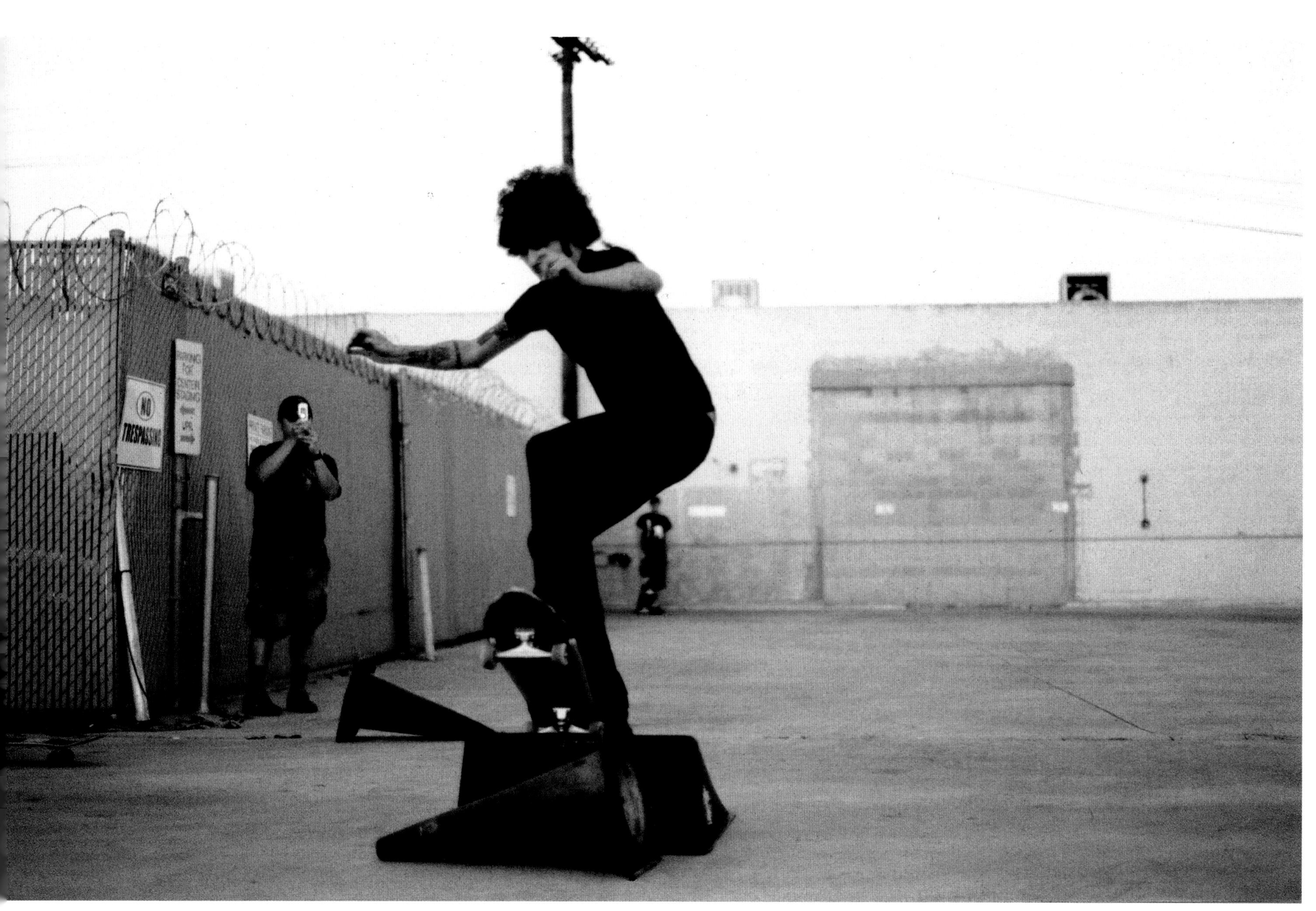
NO
TRESPASSING

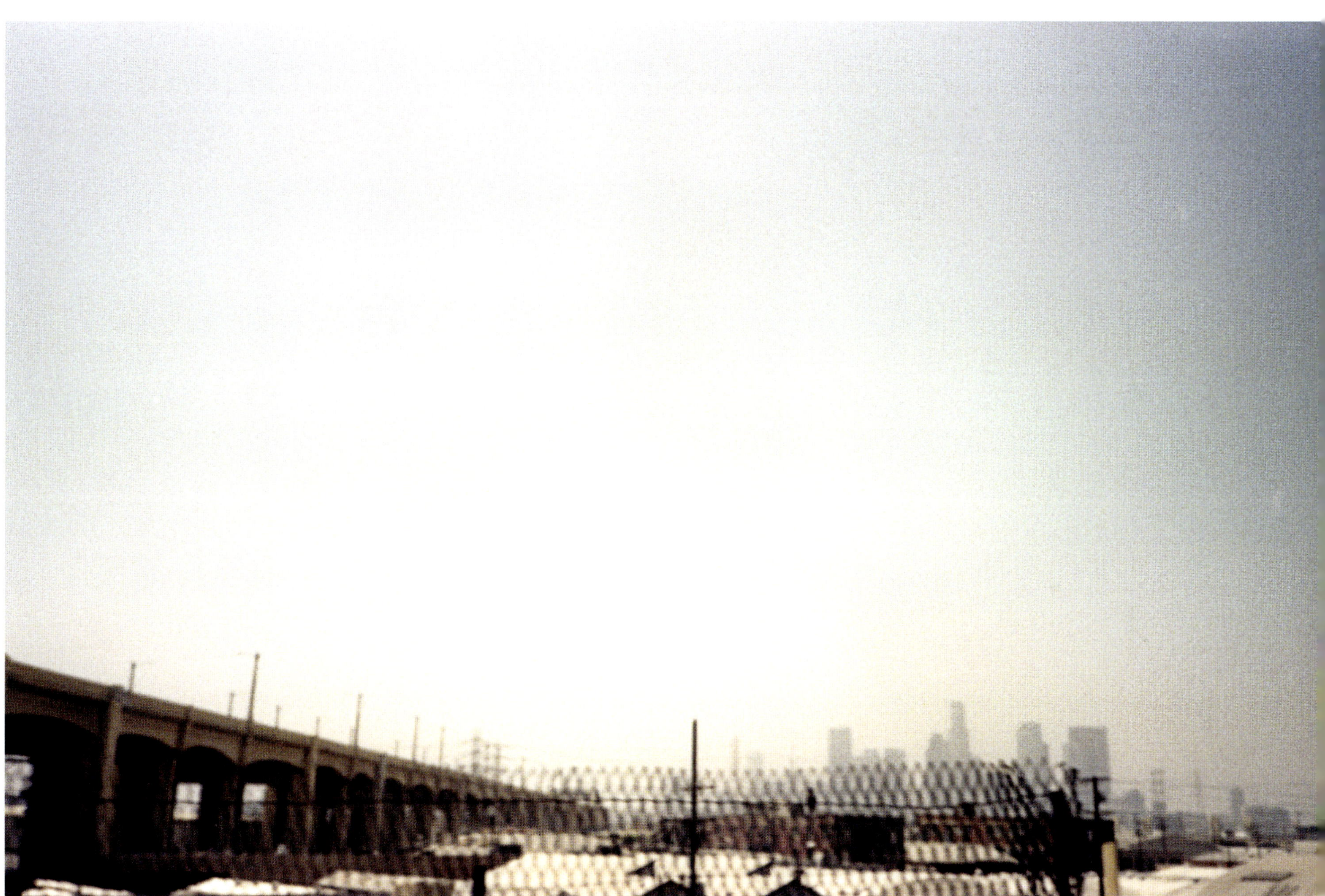

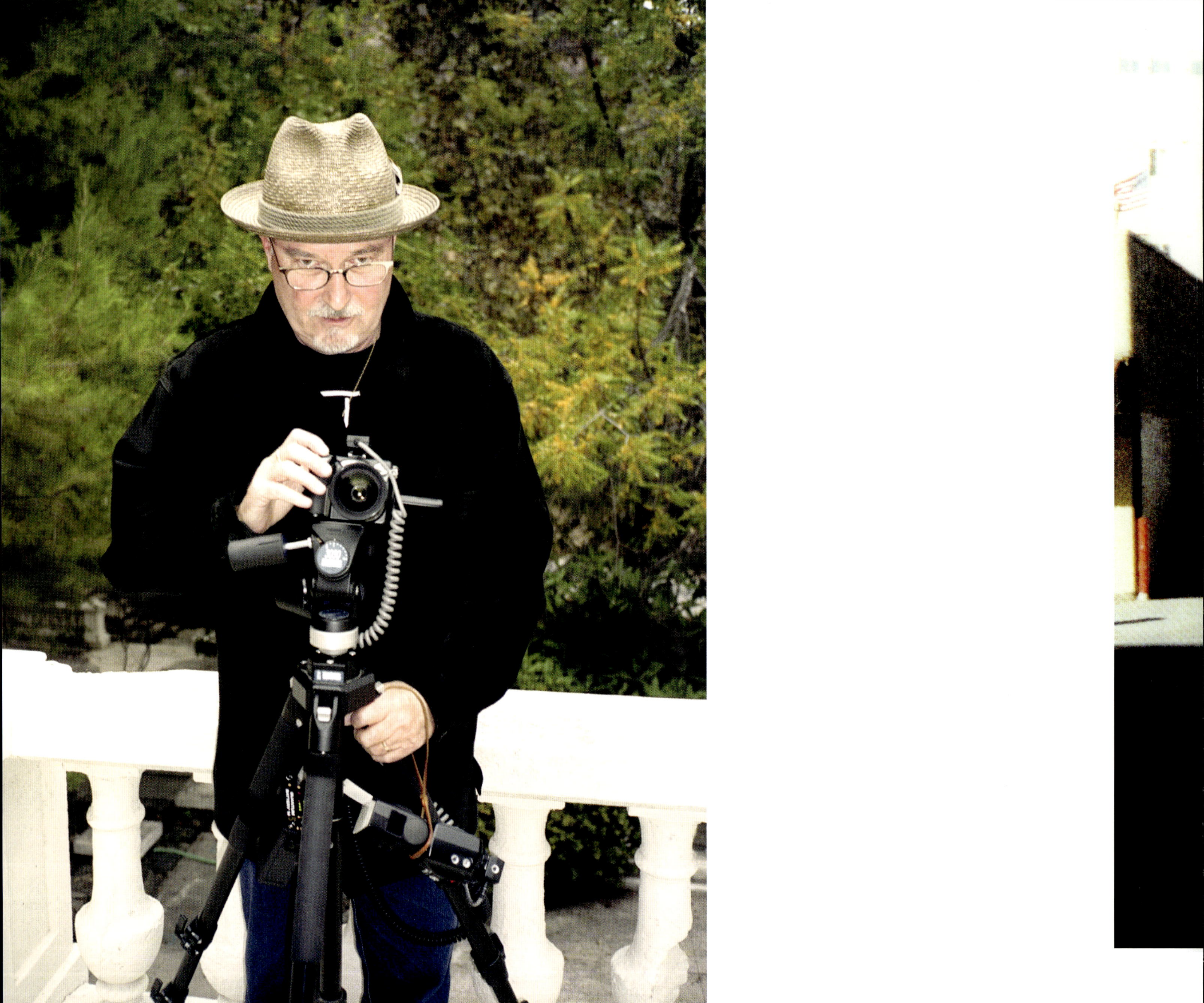

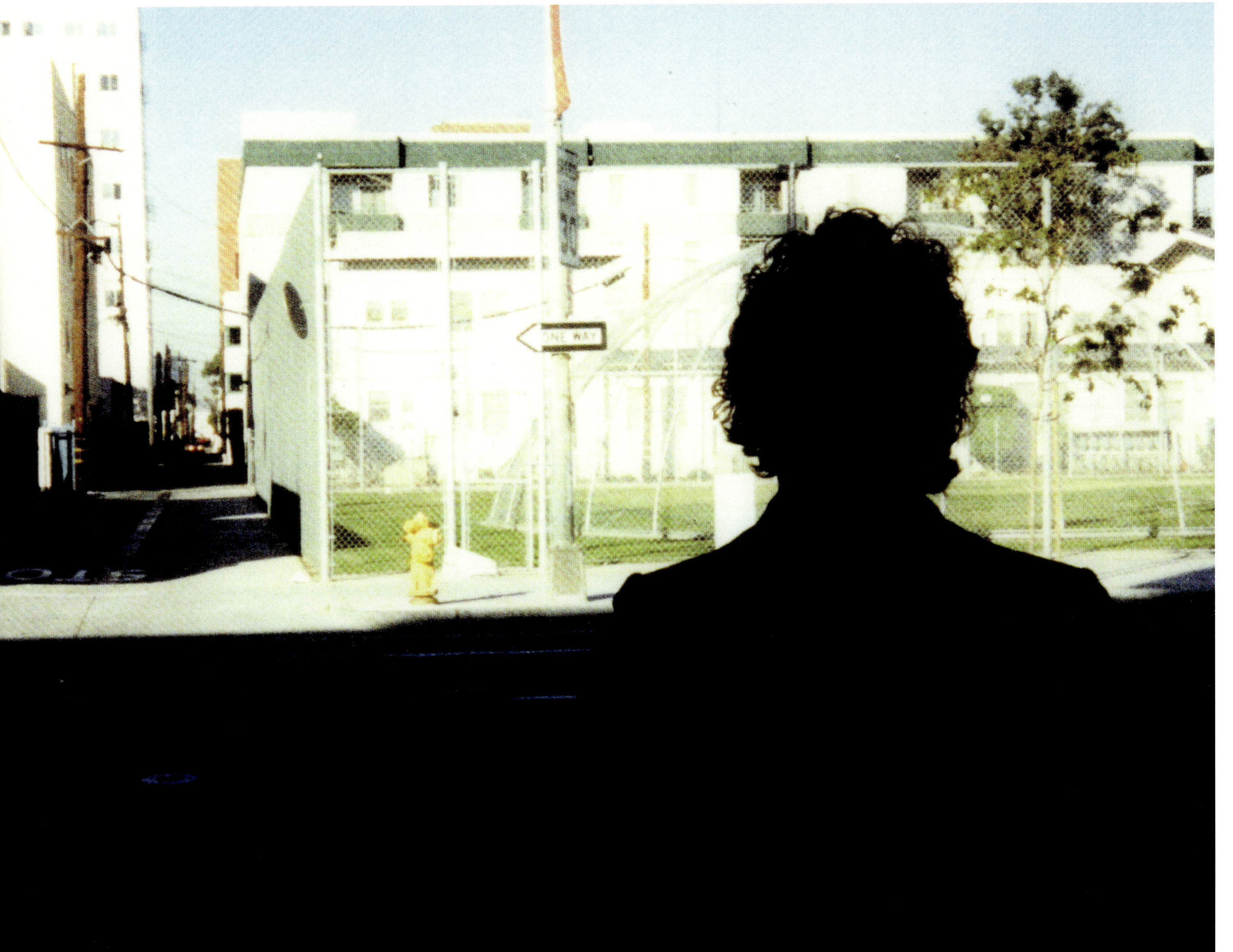
ONE WAY

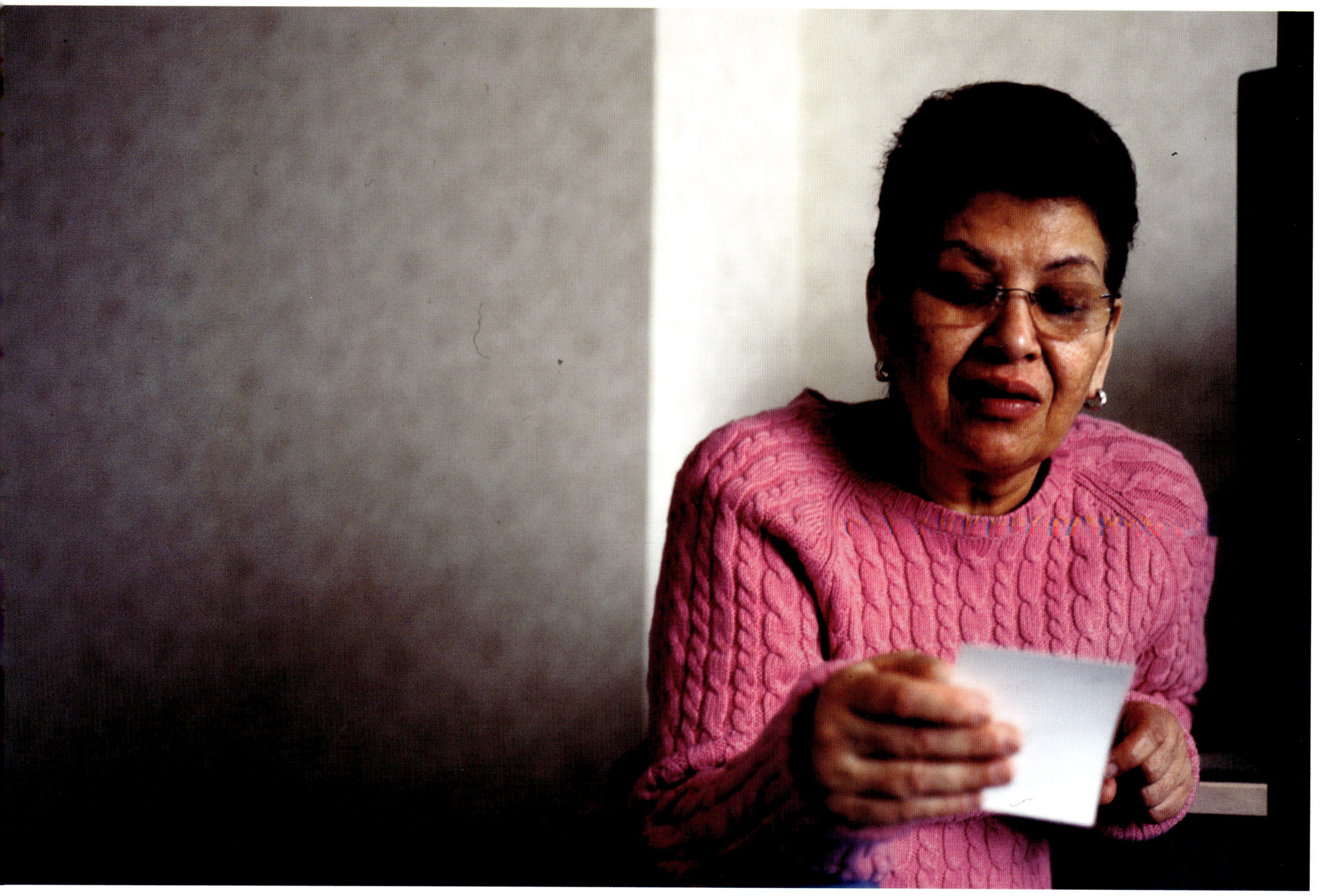

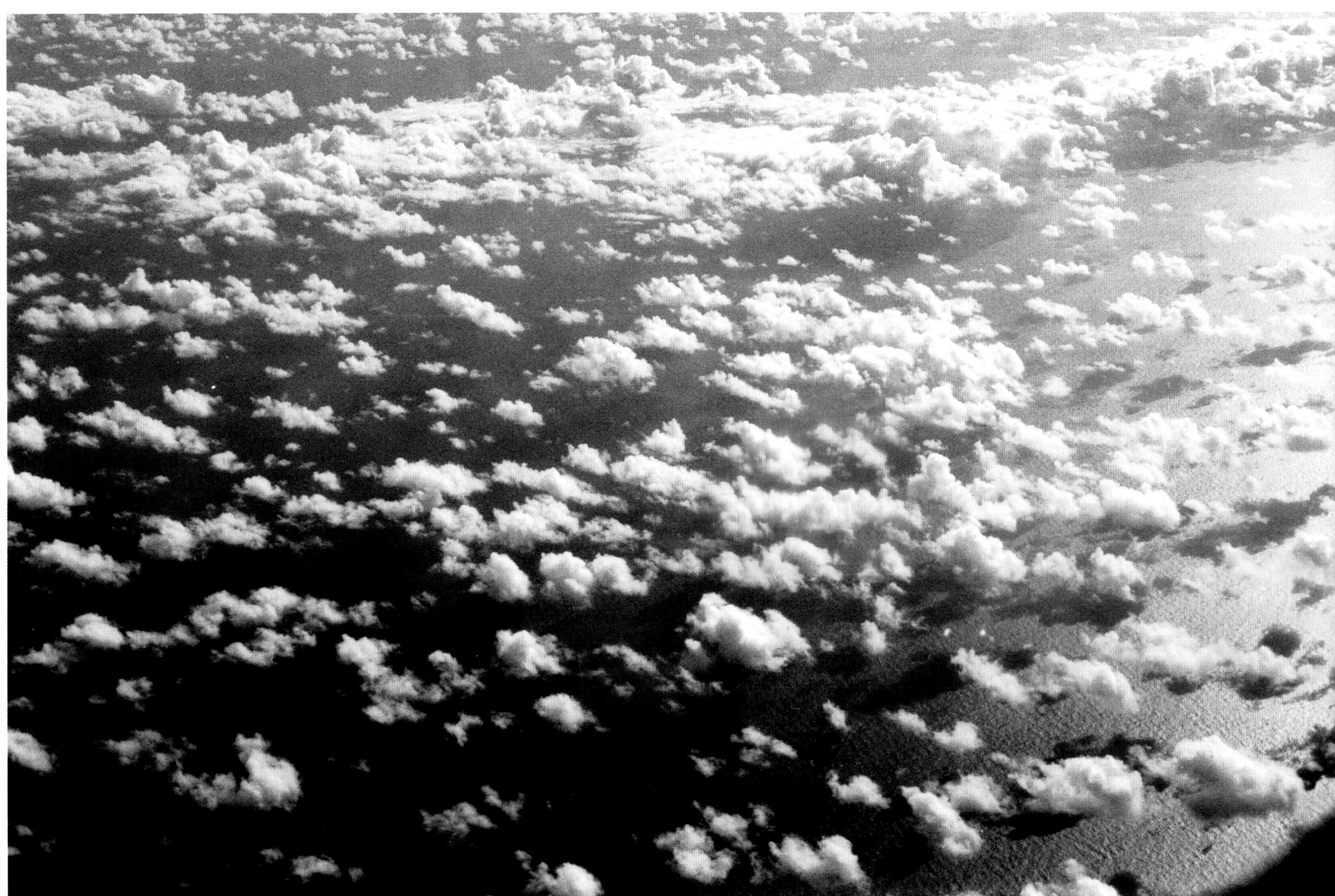

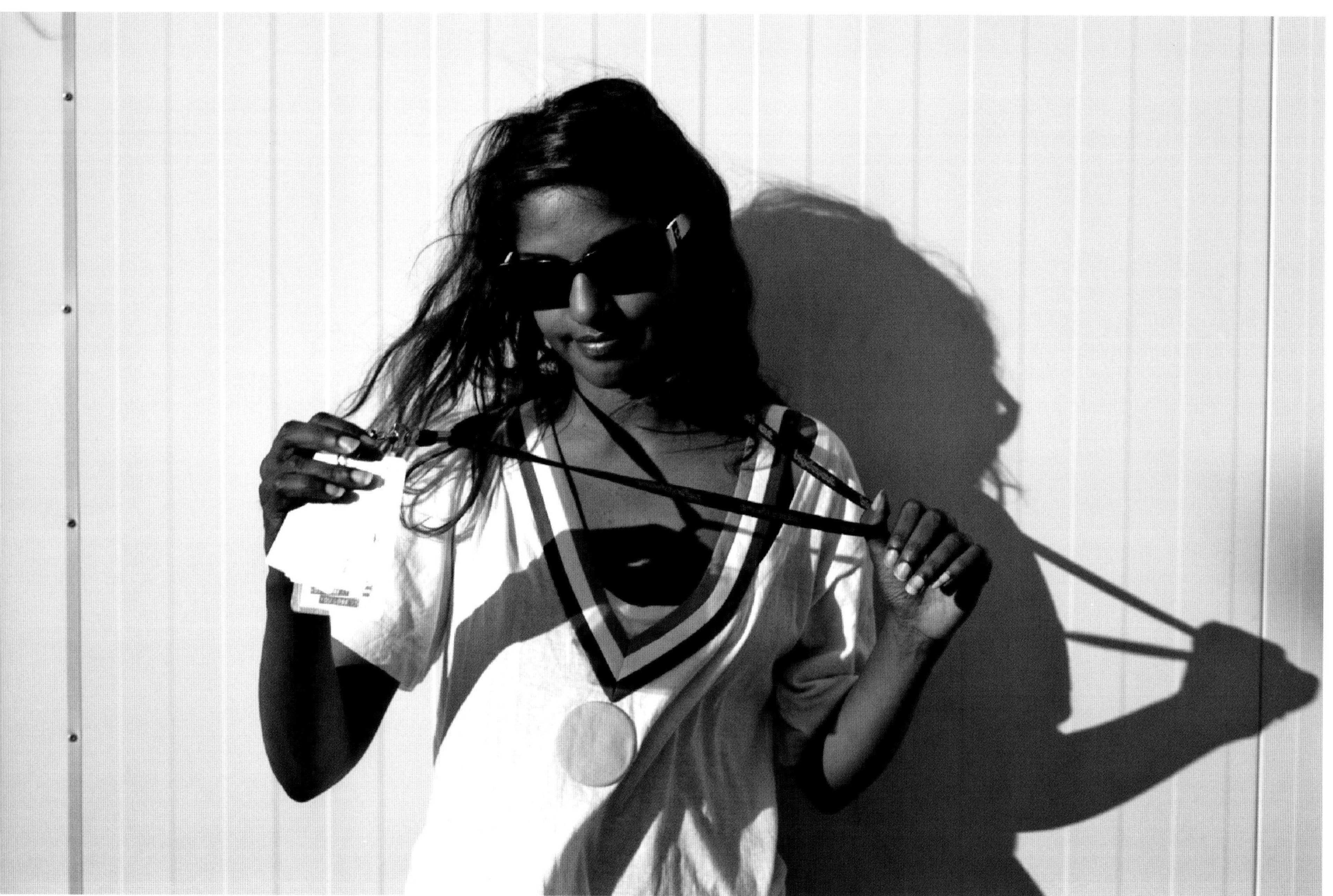

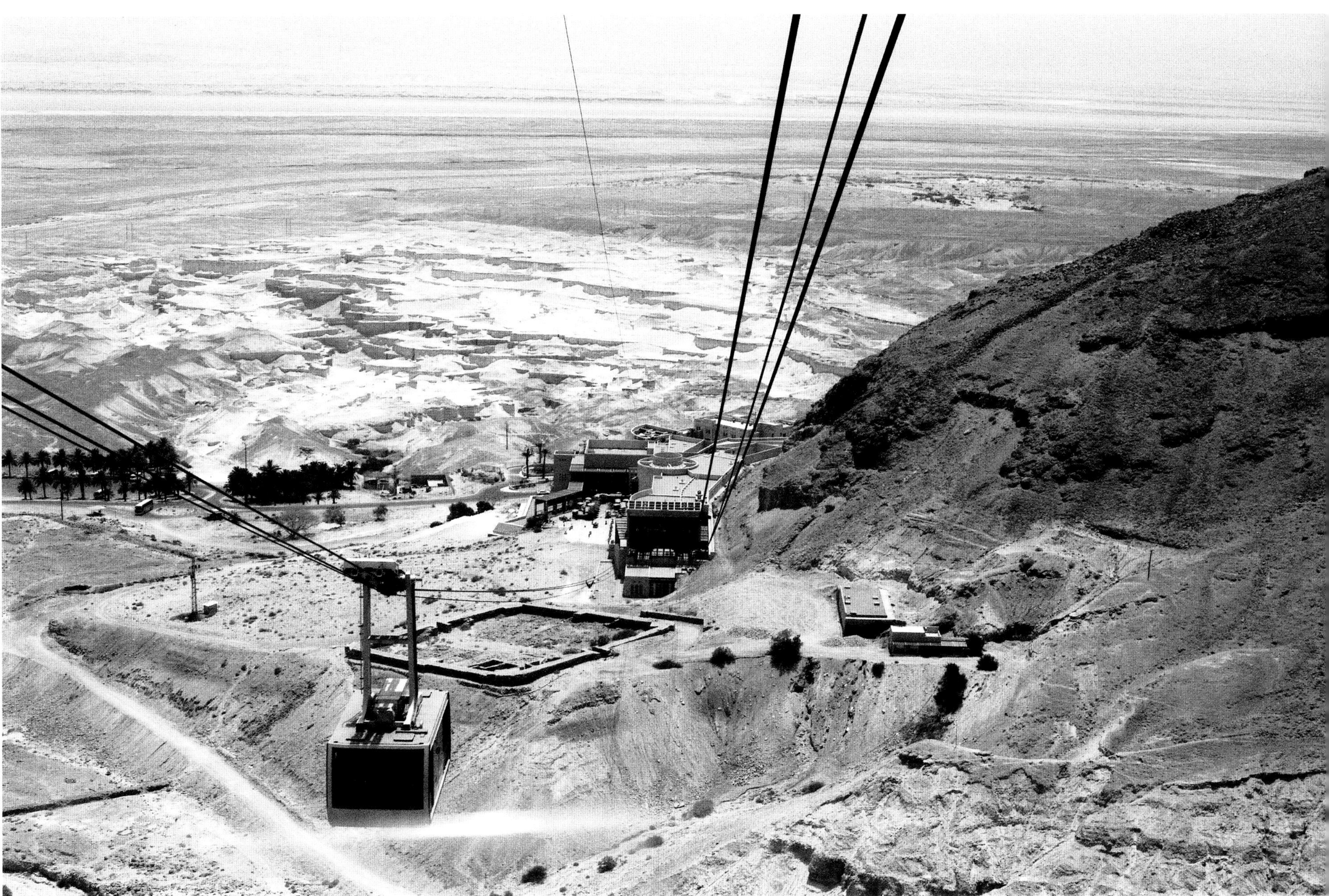

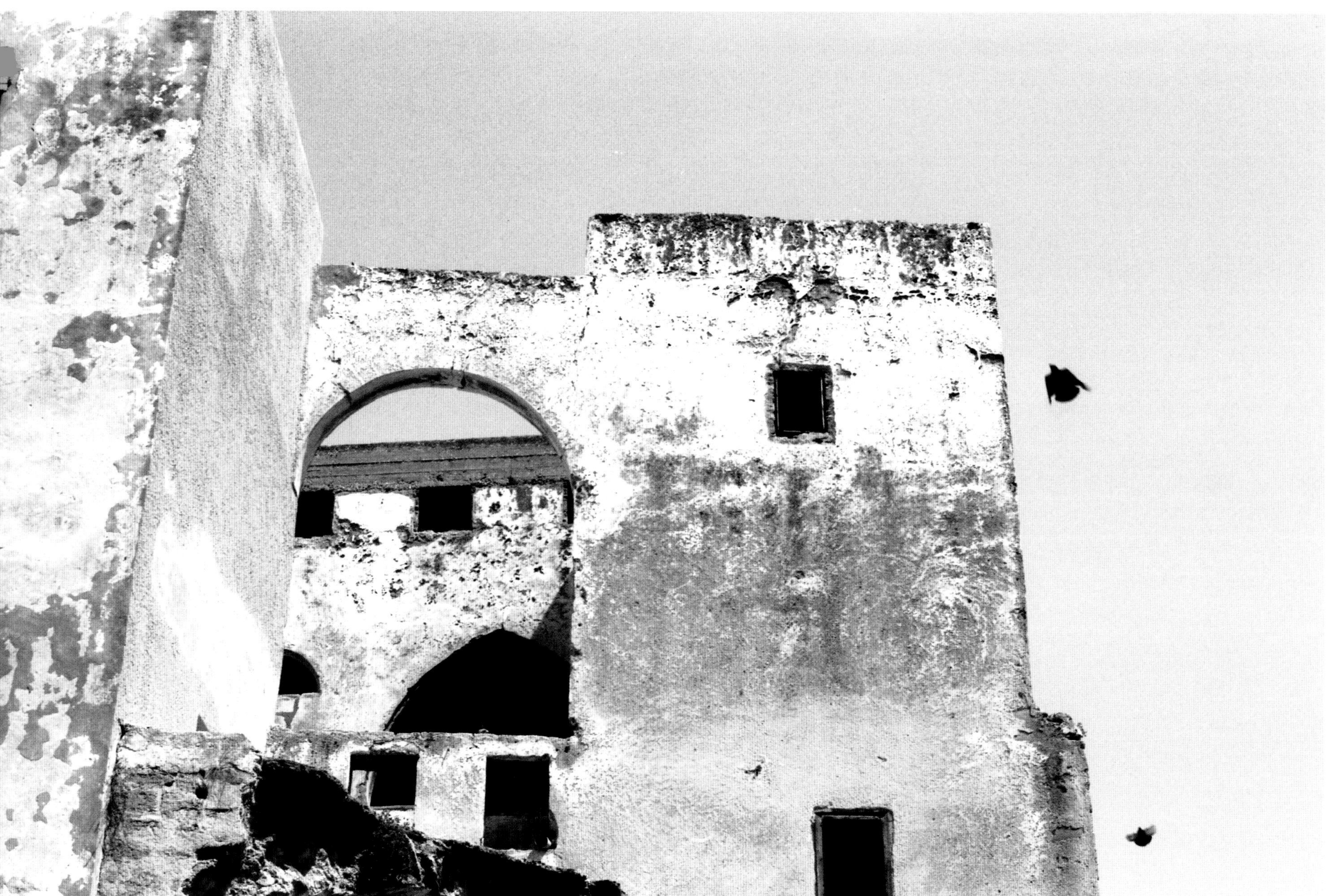

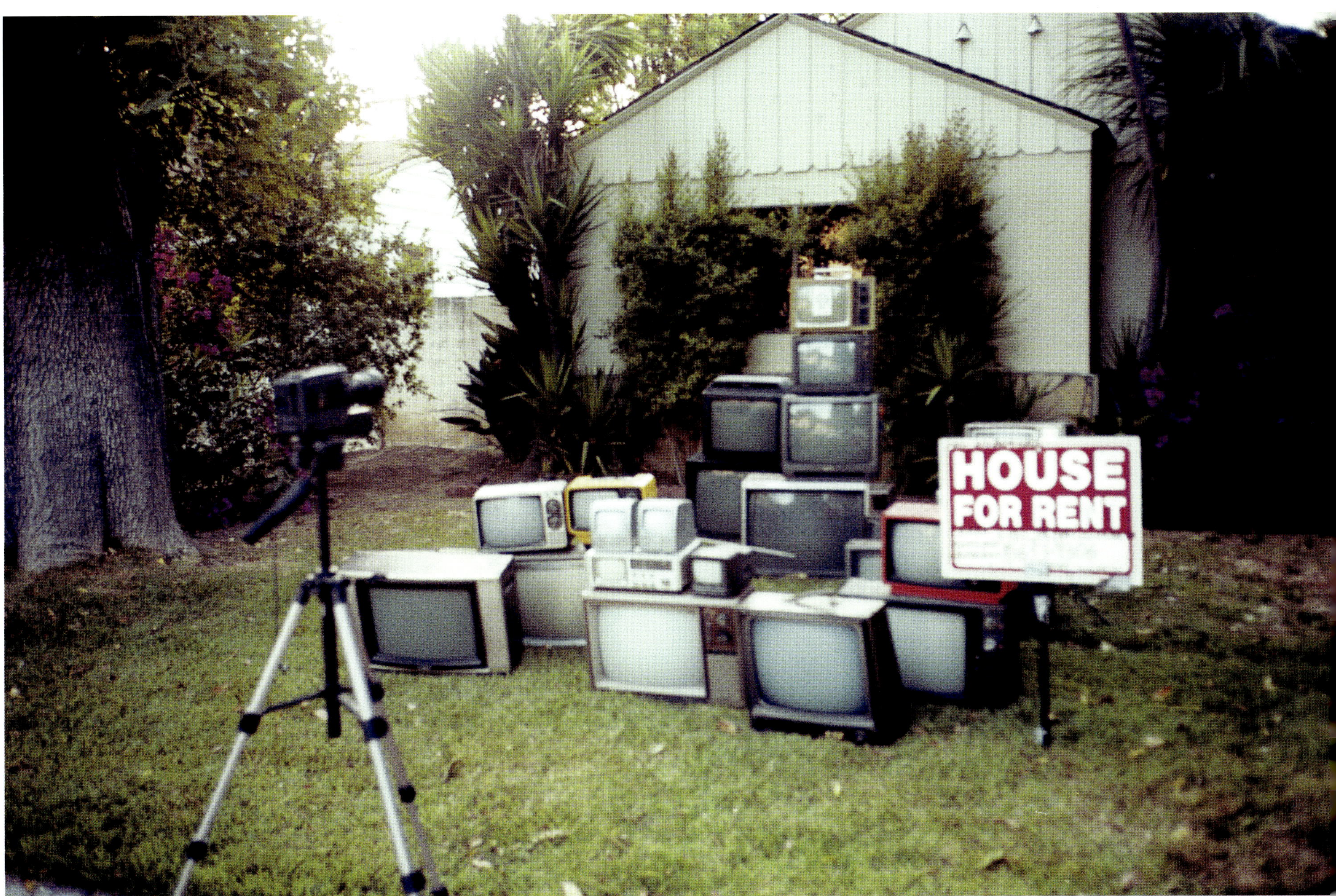
HOUSE
FOR RENT

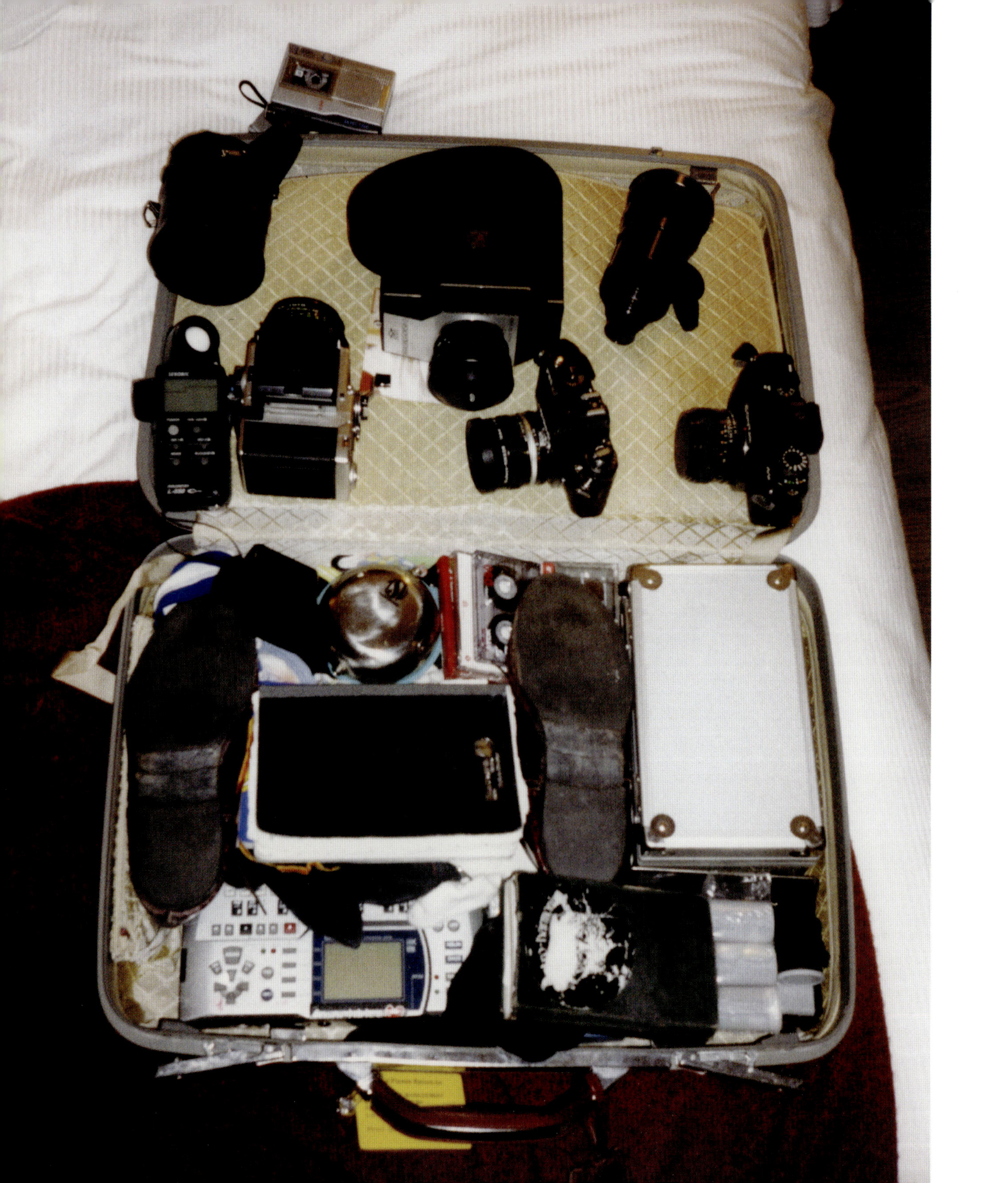

Published by Akashic Books

ISBN: 978-1-63614-210-4
Library of Congress Control Number: 2024940595

Edited by Steph Celaya
Cover design by Matthew Ortega
Book design by Jesi Maakad

First printing
Printed in China

Akashic Books
Brooklyn, New York
Instagram, X, Facebook: AkashicBooks
info@akashicbooks.com
www.akashicbooks.com